# WORLD WAR II CHRONICLES

# VICTORY IN THE PACIFIC

**MICHAEL AND GLADYS GREEN**

Series Editor: Lieutenant Colonel Roger Cirillo, United States Army, Retired

MetroBooks

# MetroBooks

An Imprint of Friedman/Fairfax Publishers

Library of Congress Cataloging-in-Publication
Green, Michael, 1952-
    Victory in the Pacific / Michael and Gladys Green
       p. cm. — (World War II chronicles)
    Includes bibliographical references and index.
    ISBN 1-56799-967-0
    1. World War, 1939-1945—Campaigns—Pacific
Area. I. Green, Gladys, 1954- II. Title.
    III. World War II chronicles (Metro Books (Firm))

    D767. V743 2000
    940.54'26—dc21
                                        00-020308

Editor: Ben Boyington
Art Director: Kevin Ullrich
Photography Editor: Erin Feller
Production Manager: Camille Lee

Color separations by Bright Arts Graphics (S) Pte
Ltd.
Printed in China by Leefung Asco Printers Ltd.

10 9 8 7 6 5 4 3 2 1

For bulk purchases and special sales, please contact:
Friedman/Fairfax Publishers
Attention: Sales Department
15 West 26th Street
New York, NY 10010
212/685-6610 FAX 212/685-1307

Visit our website:
www.metrobooks.com

## Dedication

To our good friend Huck Hagenbuch for all his help and support during the completion of this book and so many others.

## Acknowledgments

Special thanks are due to the Aircraft Carrier Hornet Foundation, the Naval Historical Center, the National Archives, the San Diego Aerospace Museum, the Marine Corps LVT Museum, and Real War Photos. Individuals who made an extra effort in helping me out on this book include Jack Green, Bob Rogers, Ray Wagner, Alex Lutz, Dick Hunnicutt, Tom Adametz, Ray Denkhaus, Frederick Pernell, and Jim Mesko. Other friends who offered their kind assistance include Ron Hare, Jacques Littlefield, Hans Halberstadt, and Milton B. Halsey, Jr.

TITLE PAGE: A geyser of water erupts behind the U.S. Navy aircraft carrier *Hornet* as a bomb from a Japanese Navy dive-bomber misses the ship during the Battle of Santa Cruz on October 26, 1942. The small black clouds that dot the skies are exploding anti-aircraft shells. In the background the *Hornet's* supporting ships also face aerial attack. Despite the intense fire aimed at the attacking Japanese aircraft, the *Hornet* was subsequently struck by two torpedoes and six bombs. Eventually, the crew was forced to abandon the badly damaged ship. Before leaving the *Hornet,* the crew scuttled it to prevent its capture by the enemy. Despite the crew's best efforts, the ship remained afloat until being sunk by four torpedoes from a passing Japanese destroyer.

LEFT: The combined power of the main guns on a U.S. Navy Iowa Class battleship is unleashed at Japanese positions in the Pacific. For shore bombardment duties, the Iowa's main guns fired a 1,900-pound (861kg) high-explosive projectile. For engaging enemy battleships or cruisers, the Iowa Class battleships employed a 2,700-pound (1,223kg) armor-piercing projectile.

# Contents

# Victory in the Pacific

## Lt. Col. Roger Cirillo (Ret.)

THE AIR RAID ON PEARL HARBOR STUNNED THE people of the United States, but the fact that Japan and the United States were on a collision course was hardly news to America's leaders. Japan's appetite for conquest had worried the United States since "the China incident" in 1931, but even before then U.S. military leaders had theorized that Japan ✗ would eventually become an enemy in the far Pacific. American war strategists had begun theoretical "contingency" plans—collectively grouped under the name "War Plan Orange"— for such a possibility as early as 1907.

The "Orange War" remained the focus of U.S. war planners for three decades, supported by the belief that a struggle over U.S. possessions in the far Pacific (such as the Philippines) might eventually erupt between the United States and the expansionist Japanese. Japanese planners, too, had seen the United States as a probable opponent, and, like the Americans, had formulated their own contingency plans.

The planners of both nations had envisioned a major action in the central Pacific, but the attack on Pearl Harbor changed all that, challenging the premises of the original Orange Plans. Made possible only because Roosevelt had transferred the Pacific Fleet to Hawaii in order to demonstrate America's resolve in the Pacific, the raid on U.S. naval interests at Pearl Harbor was settled upon by Japan's Admiral Yamamoto as the only way to

Japan's Emperor Hirohito, who ascended the throne in 1926, was a constitutional monarch with powers that were theoretically absolute. In reality, his power was very limited. He generally performed only a ceremonial role in government before and during World War II. It was only as his country faced certain defeat in late 1945 that he exerted his limited influence to bring an end to the conflict.

rapidly achieve a favorable decision in the inevitable conflict. After the U.S. fleet's rebound at the battles of Coral Sea and Midway, followed by the blocking of Japanese expansion in the Solomon Islands and New Guinea campaigns, of course, the situation

required major reevaluation on the part of the Japanese.

Pacific War strategy proved to be controversial within the halls of power. While the Allied Combined Chiefs haggled over the strategy in Europe, direction in the Pacific theater essentially rested with the American Joint Chiefs in Washington. Not surprisingly, the U.S. Army and Navy differed over strategy. The army sought to avenge and liberate the Philippines, where thousands of soldiers had been lost and millions of Filipinos, all American subjects, had been abandoned. The navy sought a marine campaign aimed at dominating the central Pacific, a gambit derived from the Orange Plans and war games of the 1920s and 1930s. That the U.S. armed forces executed both options is as much a reflection of the massive industrial and manpower resources of the United States as it was testimony to the unwillingness of President Roosevelt to curb either branch of the military or to give unqualified support to the European campaign (as Allied strategy called for).

The Pacific campaign—which was, after all, a war of vengeance—played well in U.S. newspapers, particularly because it was easily served by the propaganda mill. Japan's outrageous conduct in China was well documented, and the editors of newsreels and magazines had little difficulty procuring film and photographs of Japanese atrocities. The "Bataan

* Preparedness to go with that did not happen. And after World War I, the horrors of war compelled U.S. citizens into a pacifist attitude. JL ⊕ The conflict was not regarded as inevitable in Japan. Japanese leaders depended on the pacifist attitude to prevail. JL

○ Such as a king or queen of England. JL

Death March" and the execution of Allied prisoners of war fanned the flames of hatred for an enemy whose earlier attack at Pearl Harbor had galvanized U.S. support for the war in the first place. While the U.S. Army Air Forces were careful to explain that the strategic bombing campaign in Europe was intended to destroy only "precision targets," the fire-bombing of Japan's cities that forced the end of the war was never seriously questioned. The explosion of two atomic bombs, now the subject of much soul-searching and great debate, was seen as the "good end" to a war that many believed would continue for years in a fight to the death on Japan's home islands.

In 1945, the Japanese were portrayed as fanatical and brutal, and were seen as an enemy worth eradicating, though by that point in the war, propaganda to that effect was unnecessary. Atrocities seemed to be the rule wherever Japan's forces fought, and the fact that few Japanese surrendered gave further credence to the widely held belief that Japan would fight to the death.

It is fair to say that no war has been fought more bitterly by the United States than the war in the Pacific, and the valor of the airmen, marines, sailors, and soldiers who fought the war has never been surpassed. That the United States chose to rebuild Japan and aid in forging her democracy, and that both nations exist today as friends, is ample testimony that the horrors of the Pacific war were endured not in vain, and that the true object of war, a better peace, was in this case achieved.

The Marines of the 47th Platoon in December 1941. Despite their determined resistance, Wake Island fell to the Japanese shortly after this photograph was taken.

✱ This is the reason for the surprised comment of a Japanese admiral, "We have awakened a sleeping giant." JL

# Introduction

# From "Infamy" to Victory

FOR THE UNITED STATES, ONE OF THE TWENTIETH century's defining moments was the Japanese attack on Pearl Harbor on December 7, 1941. Prior to that day, the American public had little interest in seeing the country involved in another major war. Even the German conquest of Western Europe and the possibility that England could be invaded failed to arouse the American people. The attack on Pearl Harbor, also known as the "Day of Infamy," changed everything. It aroused a spirit of willing sacrifice and determined effort in the American people; it led to a desire for all-out war with Japan—with "unconditional surrender" as the final objective.

Because Germany and Italy had sided with the empire of Japan before its attack on Pearl Harbor, the United States was plunged overnight into a global conflict that would force it to fight on two distant fronts, even though the U.S. Army and its air forces were badly prepared to wage a large-scale war. America's political and military leaders never wavered in their determination to destroy the enemy as soon as possible. Because America was unable to deploy sufficient military forces to mount offensive operations against both Japan and its Axis allies simultaneously, however, the country's leaders decided in late December 1941 that Germany was the number one enemy. The defeat of Japan was made a secondary objective.

Despite America's focus on defeating Germany first, minor offensive operations were undertaken against Japanese military forces in early 1942. However, the major effort of the United States in the Pacific in the opening months of that year went into the development and strengthening of the lines of communications across the southern Pacific to Australia. The serious losses among Japanese planes and ships at the battles of the Coral Sea and Midway in mid-1942 redressed the naval balance of power in the Pacific and immobilized the remaining carrier striking forces of the Japanese fleet for almost two years. American shipyards and factories would use this time to build the largest and most powerful naval force ever to sail the world's oceans. In the fall and winter of 1943–1944, in conjunction with an enlarged and strengthened U.S. Army and Marine Corps, this new navy would begin a two-pronged offensive that would, by early 1945, take them to the Japanese home islands—and victory in the Pacific.

The vast expanse of the Pacific Ocean and the surrounding areas the Americans and Japanese fought over between December 7, 1941, and September 1945 is clearly evident in this simplified map. Also shown are the offensive advances made by American forces beginning in 1942 to push the Japanese back to their home islands.

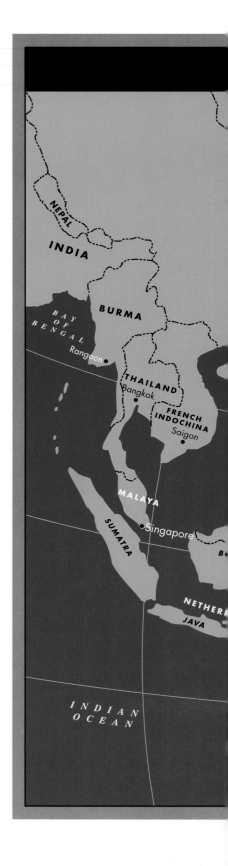

## Allied Advances in the Pacific

SOVIET UNION

MANCHURIA

JEHOL

Vladivostok

Tsingtao

KOREA

Hiroshima
Nagasaki

Shanghai

SEA OF JAPAN

JAPAN

Tokyo
DOOLITTLE RAID

Okinawa

Hong Kong

FORMOSA

Iwo Jima

PACIFIC OCEAN

BATTLE OF MIDWAY
Midway

HAWAIIAN ISLANDS

Pearl Harbor

Luzon

PHILIPPINE SEA

Manila

PHILIPPINES

Saipan

MARIANA ISLANDS

Wake

Leyte Gulf

Guam

BATTLE OF THE PHILIPPINE SEA

Eniwetok

Kwajalein

MARSHALL ISLANDS

NIMITZ'S CENTRAL PACIFIC ADVANCE

PALAU ISLANDS

Peleliu

Truk

CAROLINE ISLANDS

Morotai

Makin

Tarawa

Equator

GILBERT ISLANDS

EAST INDIES

BATTLE OF THE BISMARCK SEA

NEW GUINEA

Bougainville

NEW BRITAIN

Rabaul

SOLOMON ISLANDS

Guadalcanal

Port Moresby

BATTLE OF THE CORAL SEA

MACARTHUR'S SOUTHWEST PACIFIC ADVANCE

CORAL SEA

GHORMLEY'S/HALSEY'S SOUTH PACIFIC ADVANCE

AUSTRALIA

Allied advances

Naval Engagements

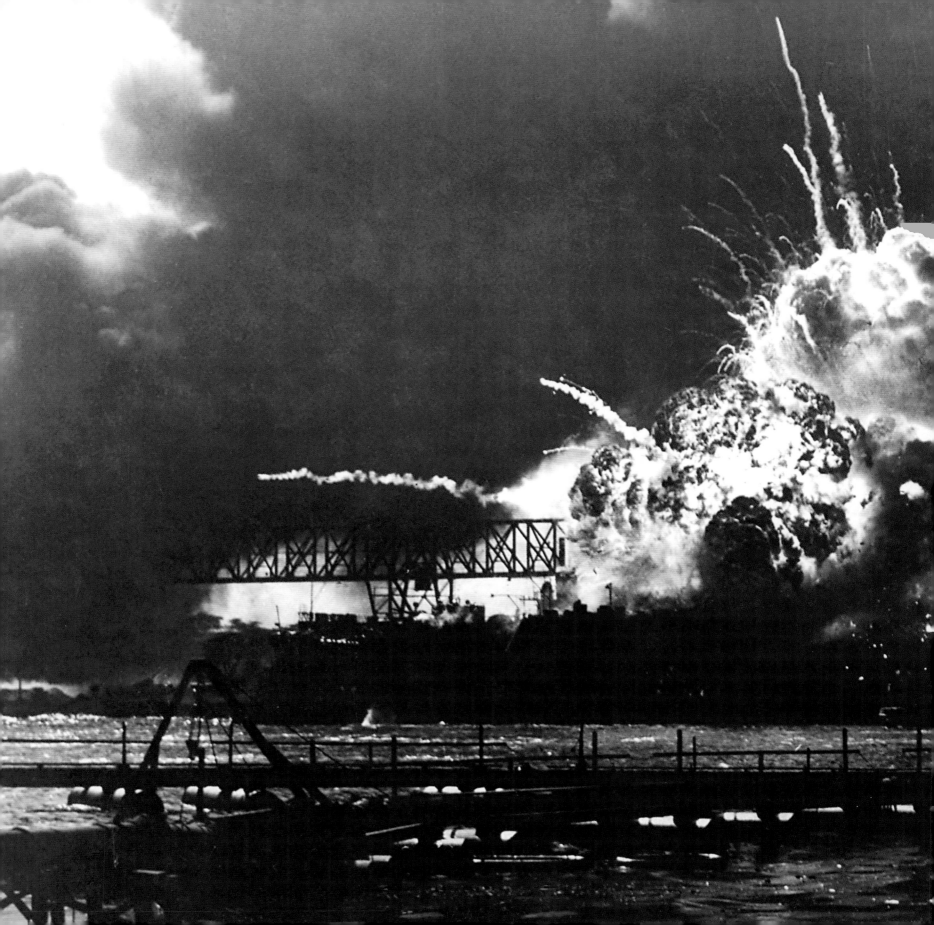

# Chapter 1

# Pearl Harbor

ON DECEMBER 7, 1941, AT PEARL HARBOR, HAWAII, THE LARGE U.S. NAVY PACIFIC Fleet was lying at anchor, smugly secure in its Pacific bastion. At 7:48 A.M. that bright Sunday morning, the commanding officer of the Kaneohe Naval Air Station was at breakfast when he noticed a formation of nine aircraft making an entrance into the bay. His son quickly pointed out that the planes bore the insignia of the Empire of Japan—the Rising Sun.

The nine planes observed by the commander and his son that Sunday morning comprised only a small fraction of the large, 184-aircraft formation that made up the first Japanese attack wave aimed at Pearl Harbor. The planes had been launched in the predawn darkness at 5:50 A.M. from Japanese Navy aircraft carriers steaming 200 miles (322km) north of Oahu. The six carriers formed the entire first-line strength of the Japanese Navy's naval air arm, under the command of Japanese Vice Admiral Chuichi Nagumo.

The six carriers and their supporting battleships, cruisers, and destroyers constituted the most powerful force of its kind ever assembled by any naval power. The Japanese Navy task force had set sail from Japan on November 27 in great secrecy. It had observed strict radio silence throughout its long journey and had made its way to America by way of the less-traveled northern Pacific to conceal its approach to the Hawaiian Islands. The destruction of the U.S. Navy Pacific Fleet was regarded as an essential element in the Japanese grand plan for conquest in the southwest Pacific, and Nagumo was under orders to carry out the mission at all costs—even if the attack was discovered by the U.S. Navy.

At 7:49 A.M. the Japanese air commander radioed his pilots to begin their attack on the unsuspecting Americans with the coded

LEFT: The U.S. Navy destroyer *USS Shaw* explodes in a massive fireball during the attack on Pearl Harbor on December 7, 1941. The *Shaw* remained afloat despite the heavy damage it sustained during the Japanese attack; it was eventually repaired and returned to service.

Pearl Harbor had been a relatively minor U.S. Navy base for many years; it did not become a major base until the early summer of 1940, as the threat from a very warlike Japan became apparent. From a military standpoint, it was not the best location. It was restricted in area and had access to the open sea in only one place. Due to its limited size, it was necessary for ships to be clustered rather than dispersed (as would usually be called for during wartime). The defenses of the base were almost nonexistent. This was a U.S. Army responsibility, but the army lacked the resources to provide much in the way of defenses, especially when it came to anti-aircraft guns and fighter aircraft.

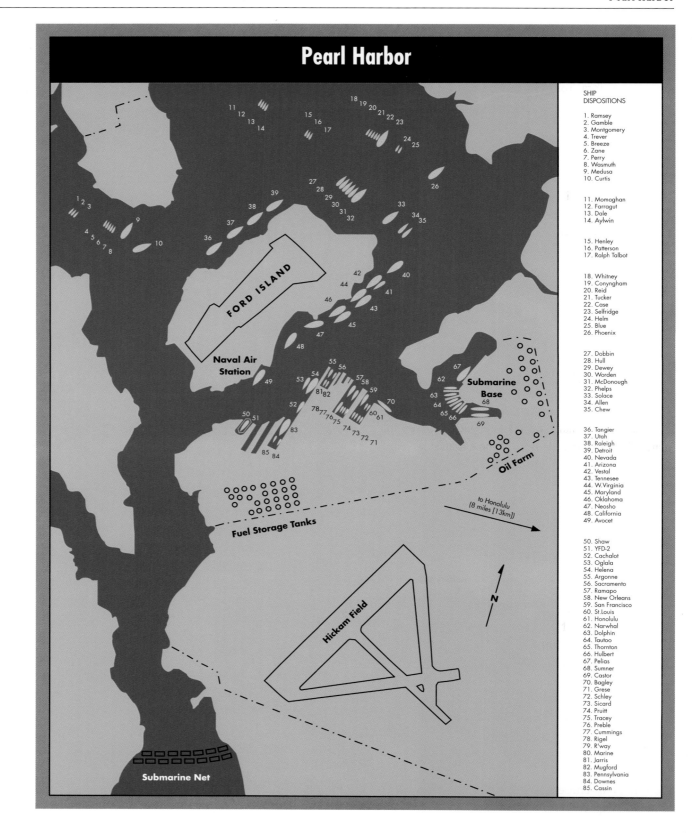

# Pearl Harbor

**SHIP DISPOSITIONS**

1. Ramsey
2. Gamble
3. Montgomery
4. Trever
5. Breeze
6. Zane
7. Perry
8. Wasmuth
9. Medusa
10. Curtis

11. Momaghan
12. Farragut
13. Dale
14. Aylwin

15. Henley
16. Patterson
17. Ralph Talbot

18. Whitney
19. Conyngham
20. Reid
21. Tucker
22. Case
23. Selfridge
24. Helm
25. Blue
26. Phoenix

27. Dobbin
28. Hull
29. Dewey
30. Worden
31. McDonough
32. Phelps
33. Solace
34. Allen
35. Chew

36. Tangier
37. Utah
38. Raleigh
39. Detroit
40. Nevada
41. Arizona
42. Vestal
43. Tennessee
44. W.Virginia
45. Maryland
46. Oklahoma
47. Neosho
48. California
49. Avocet

50. Shaw
51. YFD-2
52. Cachalot
53. Oglala
54. Helena
55. Argonne
56. Sacramento
57. Ramapo
58. New Orleans
59. San Francisco
60. St.Louis
61. Honolulu
62. Narwhal
63. Dolphin
64. Tautoo
65. Thornton
66. Hulbert
67. Pelias
68. Sumner
69. Castor
70. Bagley
71. Grese
72. Schley
73. Sicard
74. Pruitt
75. Tracey
76. Preble
77. Cummings
78. Rigel
79. R'way
80. Marine
81. Jarris
82. Mugford
83. Pennsylvania
84. Downes
85. Cassin

message "To-To-To," meaning "Charge, Charge, Charge!" Minutes later the Japanese air commander's radio operator tapped a coded message back to Admiral Nagumo—"Tora, Tora, Tora," meaning "Tiger, Tiger, Tiger!" This signified that the Japanese aerial armada had completely surprised the U.S. Navy Pacific Fleet lying in Pearl Harbor.

The fact that the Japanese attack on Pearl Harbor came as a complete surprise to the American military, despite much warning from a variety of sources, was the result of a series of tactical errors and failures. Seemingly endless rounds of wartime and postwar investigations attempted to apportion blame for the Pearl Harbor disaster. All investigations concluded that the entire American military chain of command (from enlisted personnel to the president) had underestimated the increasingly apparent threat posed by the warlike posturing of the military-dominated Japanese government in the months preceding the attack on Pearl Harbor.

On the very day of the attack, the American command structure at Pearl Harbor failed to respond to signs that an enemy assault was imminent. The first clue was the sinking of a small, two-man midget Japanese submarine by the destroyer *Ward* at the entrance to Pearl Harbor at 6:53 A.M. on the morning of December 7. High-ranking officers at Pearl Harbor dismissed the report as the product of overanxious young sailors who were seeing things that did not exist.

A second suspicious event occurred at 7:02 A.M., when a U.S. Army radar unit on the northern tip of Oahu detected Japanese planes 137 miles (220km) north of the island. This report was dismissed as a misidentification of returning American planes.

Since the U.S. Navy's three Pacific Fleet aircraft carriers were not in port on December 7, the primary Japanese targets were the Pacific Fleet's eight battleships—*California, Maryland, Oklahoma, West Virginia, Tennessee, Arizona, Nevada,* and *Pennsylvania.* Seven of the ships were anchored close together alongside Ford Island in the center of Pearl Harbor. The *Pennsylvania* was in dry dock.

The other eighty-six U.S. Navy ships in the harbor, including nine cruisers, twenty-nine destroyers, and numerous support vessels, were clustered together in

a very small area. The Japanese naval aviator in charge of the Pearl Harbor attack would later remark that he could not believe that the U.S. Navy would make its ships such easy targets.

The suddenness of the Japanese attack left the battleship anti-aircraft gun crews with no time to react before bombs and torpedoes hit their targets. With only skeleton crews on board and no advance warning, the battleships proved easy targets. The *Arizona* exploded and sank. The *Oklahoma* capsized. The *West Virginia* and the *California* sank. The *Nevada* was beached. The *Maryland* and the *Tennessee*, moored inboard of the other battleships, sustained only light to moderate damage from the bombs dropped. The dry-docked *Pennsylvania* was hit by only one bomb.

A pre-World War II aerial view of the extensive dry-dock and ship-repair facilities at the U.S. Navy base at Pearl Harbor. The Japanese failure to destroy the machine shops located in this area during their attack on December 7, 1941, was a serious mistake. It allowed the U.S. Navy to repair its warships at a much faster rate than if they had been forced to return the ships to the West Coast of the United States.

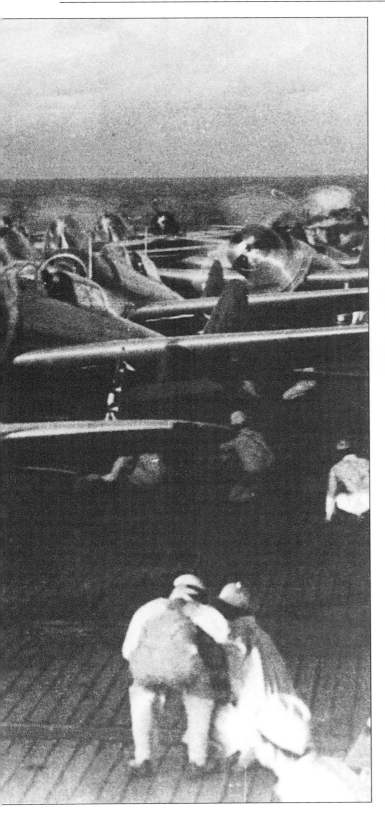

## The Japanese Attack Continues

The first Japanese attack wave of 184 planes was in the air over Pearl Harbor for about fifty minutes before returning to the carriers. The Japanese lost only nine planes in this first attack. The second wave of 170 aircraft was launched while the first was still moving toward Pearl Harbor. The second wave arrived over Pearl Harbor at 8:40 A.M., not long after the first wave left.

During the brief lull between attacks, the Americans feverishly prepared for the second aerial assault they knew was coming. As a result, the second wave of Japanese planes was confronted with heavy anti-aircraft fire from the surviving ships and ground positions. Also, large black smoke clouds from the burning ships obscured the entire target area. Despite these obstacles, the Japanese pilots were able to do further damage to the moored battleships, as well as to a number of cruisers and destroyers.

The second wave of attacking Japanese planes managed to damage the battleship *Nevada* on its escape toward the open sea. To avoid blocking the narrow

OPPOSITE: Japanese pilots on the wooden flight deck of an aircraft carrier await the signal to launch. When the signal is given, the flight deck personnel will remove the wheel blocks, allowing the aircraft to roll forward. At the time, Japanese pilots were probably the most experienced in the world due to extensive combat action in China during the 1930s and early 1940s. ABOVE: This very rare wartime propaganda shot shows the two-man flight crew inside a Japanese Navy Aichi D3A dive-bomber, called the "Val." The Val played an important role during the Japanese attack on Pearl Harbor; it was used to sink more Allied ships than any other aircraft used in the war.

RIGHT: Explosions and dark black smoke dominate the sky above American sailors stationed on Ford Island during the Japanese attack on Pearl Harbor. The rear of a twin-engine Consolidated PBY flying boat and a number of single-engine Vought OS2U Kingfisher seaplanes can be seen among the wreckage.

OPPOSITE, TOP: This famous picture taken by an American sailor during the Japanese attack on Pearl Harbor shows six of the Navy's battleships berthed along battleship row, which was adjacent to Ford Island. The billowing clouds of smoke are coming from the battleship *Arizona*, which was struck by at least one torpedo and at least eight bombs. One of the bombs penetrated the front of the ship and landed in an ammunition storage room. The resulting explosion broke the ship in half, and many lives were lost.

OPPOSITE, BOTTOM: An American soldier examines the remains of a U.S. Army Air Corps Curtiss P-40 Warhawk fighter destroyed on Wheeler Field during the Japanese attack on Pearl Harbor. At the time, the Warhawk was the essential fighter in the American military inventory. Because of the fear of local sabotage, the Japanese attackers found the American fighter planes arranged in nice neat rows for easy destruction.

channel that led to the sea, the captain of the *Nevada* ordered his ship run aground. By 9:45 A.M. the Japanese pilots were low on fuel and ammunition, and they returned to their carriers. Losses for the second Japanese wave totaled only twenty aircraft.

By the time the second wave of Japanese planes had returned to the carriers, the aircraft assigned to the first wave had been refueled and rearmed for a third attack. This time, the primary targets were the U.S. Navy's large fuel storage tanks and ship-repair facilities. Destruction of these targets would add many months to the redeployment of the Pacific Fleet. It was at this important point that the Japanese carrier commander, Admiral Nagumo, made a critical error in judgment.

Nagumo was convinced that American land-based planes were still capable of launching an attack on his prized carriers. He therefore erred on the side of caution,

canceled the third air attack, and ordered his ships to return to Japan. His peers would later criticize him for his lack of aggression at this key moment. American Admiral Chester W. Nimitz summarized Nagumo's decision:

*Future students of our naval war in the Pacific will inevitably conclude that the Japanese commander of the carrier task force missed a golden opportunity in restricting his attack on Pearl Harbor to one day's operation, and in the very limited choice of objectives.*

All eight of the Navy's Pacific Fleet battleships were knocked out of action in the Pearl Harbor attack. All but the *Arizona* and the *Oklahoma* were returned to service during the war. The Japanese attackers also sank the cruiser *Raleigh*, which was later repaired and returned to service. Two other cruisers, the *Helena* and the *Honolulu*, escaped with only light damage. The destroyers *Cassin*, *Shaw*, and *Downes* were all severely damaged during the attack, but all were eventually returned to service. Crew losses among the various ships amounted to 1,763 officers and men. Including the losses from land-based military and civilian personnel, the number of Americans killed at Pearl Harbor on December 7 totaled 2,335, with another 1,735 wounded.

The various military airfields on the island of Oahu were important secondary targets for the Japanese pilots involved in the attack on Pearl Harbor. The two most important were Hickam and Wheeler. With little effort, the Japanese managed to destroy ninety-six of the 231 American military aircraft at Pearl Harbor on December 7. The planes were also easy targets. Due to fear of sabotage by Japanese agents, all military planes on the island of Oahu were parked closely together; this made it easier to guard them. Only a handful of American planes left the ground during the Japanese attack.

Eight hours after their successful attack on Pearl Harbor, the Japanese government officially declared war on the United States. The Japanese prime minister, General Hideki Tojo, issued a statement in the name of the Emperor Hirohito:

> *Men and officers of our Army and Navy shall do their utmost in prosecuting the war . . . . [T]he entire nation, with united will, shall mobilize their total strength so that nothing will miscarry in the attainment of our war aims . . . .*
>
> *Eager for the realization of their inordinate ambition to dominate the Orient, both America and Britain . . . have aggravated the disturbances in East Asia. Moreover, these two powers, inducing other countries to follow suit, increased military preparations on all sides of our Empire to challenge us. They have obstructed by every means our peaceful commerce, and finally have resorted to the direct severance of economic relations, menacing gravely the existence of our Empire . . . .*
>
> *The situation being such as it is, our Empire, for its existence and self-defense, has no other recourse but to appeal to arms and to crush every obstacle in its path . . . .*

# Battleships

A battleship is a large, heavily armored floating gun platform designed to engage and sink any type of enemy ship by long-range gunfire. For U.S. Navy battleships during World War II, the main armament normally consisted of nine to twelve large-caliber, direct-fire guns with a range of 12 to 24 miles (19–38km).

These battleships ranged in displacement from 27,000 to 52,000 tons (24,300–46,800t). Length averaged between 573 and 880 feet (175–268m) with a maximum width of 100 feet (30m). They had a top speed of 21 to 32 knots. Crew complements could range from 1,000 to 2,000 men.

Before the United States entered World War II following the surprise attack on Pearl Harbor, the top brass of the U.S. Navy had considered the battleship the key ship in the fleet. Aircraft carriers played only a supporting role, assisting the battleships in locating the enemy's fleet. With the loss of so many battleships at Pearl Harbor, however, the Navy was forced to use the aircraft carrier as the main ship of the fleet. Aircraft carriers would prove so effective in this new role that, even when new and improved battleships entered fleet service, they were quickly relegated to the role of antiaircraft support ships for the carriers or shore bombardment vessels.

USS *California* (BB-44)

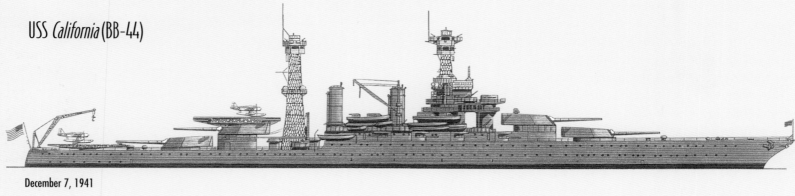

December 7, 1941

September 2, 1945

ABOVE: Sunk during the Japanese attack on Pearl Harbor, the battleship *California* (top) was refloated by the U.S. Navy in March 1942. After some initial repairs were completed at Pearl Harbor to make the ship seaworthy, it set sail for Bremerton, Washington, where it was to undergo more extensive repairs. The *California* was returned to Pacific Fleet service in early 1944 (bottom) and saw heavy action during the remainder of the war. Reflecting the growing importance of electronic warfare to the U.S. Navy during World War II, the reconstructed *California* was fitted with a wide array of different types of new radar units.
OPPOSITE: The crew of the U.S. Navy battleship *California* abandons the listing ship as burning oil from other stricken vessels berthed along battleship row engulfs her. Two torpedoes and one aerial bomb struck the *California* during the Japanese attack. Due to counter flooding (a practice undertaken to prevent the ship from tipping over) by the ship's crew prior to its abandonment, it eventually settled into the shallow mud of Pearl Harbor more or less upright.

In the foreground is the upturned hull of the U.S. Navy battleship *Oklahoma*, which took four Japanese torpedo hits in quick succession during the first few moments of the Japanese attack on Pearl Harbor. The battleship *Maryland*, in the background, was protected from enemy torpedoes because she was berthed between the shore and the *Oklahoma*.

The reference to the direct severance of economic relations referred to the American trade embargo instituted by President Franklin D. Roosevelt in July 1941. This embargo effectively cut off the oil Japan needed for its industrial and military forces. President Roosevelt also ordered that Japanese assets in the United States be frozen. Both these measures were taken as a form of diplomatic punishment to express the president's continued unhappiness with Japanese military aggression in China, which had started in 1931.

Japan's displeasure with the trade embargo, and the seriousness with which the Japanese regarded the action, is apparent in the prewar statement of a high-ranking Japanese civilian official: "If the present condition is left unchecked . . . Japan will find itself totally exhausted and unable to rise in the future."

Japan's leaders were convinced that the American trade embargo would bring about their nation's complete collapse within two years. For many of Japan's political and military leaders, the only recourse open to them in the face of the embargo was to go to war with the United

States while their country still had the power to do so. In a 1949 interview, a member of the Japanese royal family stated that "Japan entered the war with a tragic determination and in desperate self-abandonment."

Shocked by the surprise attack on Pearl Harbor, the American public suddenly changed its long-standing aversion to U.S. military participation in World War II and demanded revenge against Japan. Reflecting the new hawkish attitude of the American people, President Roosevelt called an emergency session of Congress on December 8 to declare war on Japan. The entire U.S. population heard his now-famous radio broadcast:

> *Yesterday, December 7, 1941—a date which will live in infamy—the United States of America was suddenly and deliberately attacked by naval and air forces of the Empire of Japan . . . . It will be recorded that the distance of Hawaii from Japan makes it obvious that the attack was deliberately planned many days or even weeks ago. During the intervening time, the Japanese government had deliberately sought to deceive the United States by false statements and expressions of hope for continued peace.*

On December 11, Adolf Hitler, under no obligation to Japan and without much thought for the long-term consequences, declared war on the United States. This put America in the unenviable position of having to fight a war across two oceans with a navy still recovering from heavy losses sustained at Pearl Harbor. Fortunately, both Roosevelt and the senior leadership of the U.S. Navy had long believed that it was inevitable that Japanese national interests in the Pacific would collide with those of the United States. Roosevelt and the navy had managed to convince a reluctant Congress to fund the construction of new warships beginning in the early 1930s.

With the successful German invasion of France in May 1940 and the growing German threat to Great Britain, Roosevelt signed the so-called Two-Ocean Bill on July 19, 1940. This bill would set into motion the largest single naval building program ever undertaken by any country. In response to the Japanese attack on Pearl Harbor, Congress poured billions of dollars into the Navy's shipbuilding budget.

In the 1930s, after the U.S. military came to believe that war with Japan was just a matter of time, the navy ordered into production a new type of fast battleship known as the Iowa Class. Six were ordered, but only four saw action in World War II. In this 1942 photograph, the first of these ships, the *Iowa*, is prepared for launching.

*.. we here highly resolve that these dead shall not have died in vain . . .*

*REMEMBER DEC. 7th!*

This popular propaganda poster clearly aimed at reminding the American people why they became involved in the conflict. Many other propaganda posters of the time appealed to the much baser racist stereotypes of American society.

of the Empire of Japan enjoyed great success in expanding their military and economic control over the Southwest Pacific as well as Southeast Asia.

With the U.S. Navy Pacific Fleet temporarily out of action, the Japanese quickly moved southward and eastward to occupy Malaya, the Dutch East Indies (now known as Indonesia), the Philippines, Wake Island, Guam, the Gilbert Islands, Thailand, and Burma. Once in control of these areas, the Japanese established a defensive perimeter stretching from the Kurile Islands south through Wake, the Marianas, the Carolines, and the Marshall and Gilbert islands to Rabaul on the large island of New Britain. From Rabaul the Japanese defensive perimeter extended westward to northwestern New Guinea and back to the Dutch East Indies, Malaya, Thailand, and Burma.

Japan's top leaders persuaded themselves that the American military would not be able to break through the defensive perimeter and, therefore, the U.S. government would settle for a negotiated peace that would leave Japan in possession of most of its conquests. However, some Japanese civilian and military officials who were more familiar with America's industrial capacity and the resolve of the U.S. population were not convinced. One of those skeptics was Grand Admiral Isoruku Yamamoto, who came up with the plan to attack Pearl Harbor. Yamamoto had studied at Harvard and later served as a naval attaché in Washington, D.C. He had formed a very positive impression of America and its people. Unlike many of his peers, he did not believe that U.S. leaders would give up the fight before a final victory was theirs.

Before the Japanese attack on Pearl Harbor was launched, Grand Admiral Yamamoto confided to a fellow admiral:

The rapid pace of the American naval expansion program, continuing through early 1943, astonished the Japanese. For every completed Japanese warship, American shipyards built sixteen. The buildup allowed the U.S. Navy to seize and hold the initiative much sooner than anticipated. However, large numbers of new warships do not appear overnight in even the most productive shipyards. Until the fruits of America's naval expansion could be placed in service, the armed forces

*If we are ordered to fight the United States we might be able to score a runaway victory and hold our own for six months or a year. But in the second year the Americans will increase their strength, and it will be very difficult for us to fight on with any prospects of final victory.*

Yamamoto was uncannily prescient in his assessment. He did not survive the war.

# The Numbers Game

Although numbers do not always indicate the true effectiveness of any type of weapon system, they can provide a basic and easy-to-understand look at the relative strength of two opposing forces.

Listed at right are the comparative numbers of warships in the U.S. and Japanese Navies on December 1, 1941, six days before the attack on Pearl Harbor. The figures in parentheses indicate warships under construction at the time.

| U.S. Navy | Japanese Navy |
| --- | --- |
| Battleships: 16 (16) | Battleships: 10 (3) |
| Aircraft Carriers: 7 (11) | Aircraft Carriers: 8 (8) |
| Cruisers: 43 (40) | Cruisers: 38 (10) |
| Destroyers: 171 (188) | Destroyers: 108 (43) |

USS *Nevada* (BB-36)

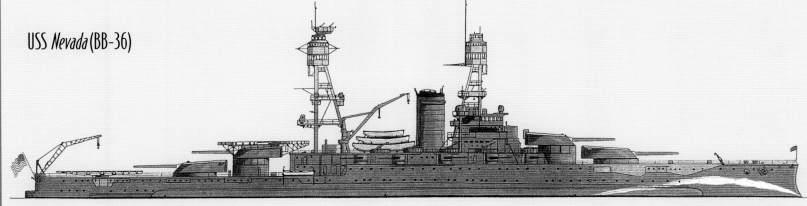

December 7, 1941

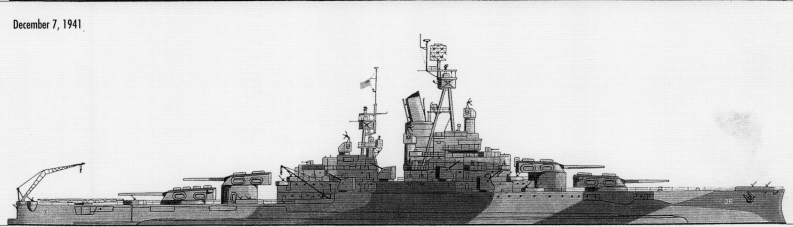

March 1944

The U.S. Navy battleship *Nevada,* beached during the Japanese attack on Pearl Harbor, was refloated in February 1942. The ship was returned to the East Coast of the United States in June 1942 to undergo a long-overdue modernization process, as depicted in these before-and-after diagrams. The job was completed in March 1944. After serving in the Atlantic for the remainder of 1944, the *Nevada* rejoined the Pacific Fleet in early 1945.

# Chapter 2

# Defeat and Victory

ONCE THE THREAT POSED BY THE U.S. NAVY PACIFIC FLEET BASED AT PEARL HARBOR was eliminated, the Japanese turned their attention to the American-controlled Philippine Islands located 2,000 miles (3,267km) south of Japan. At the time, the only major American military outpost in the Southwest Pacific was located in the Philippines. Before the Japanese could benefit from the rich natural resources of the Dutch East Indies (Indonesia) and Malaya, they would have to neutralize the Philippines.

Of the 7,000 islands that make up the Philippines, the largest and most populous is Luzon. In late 1941, Luzon was home to most of the American military forces based in the Philippines. The American and Philippine armed forces were under the command of America's best-known military hero from World War I, General Douglas MacArthur.

The Japanese battle plan for the Philippines included, as a first priority, the destruction of MacArthur's land-based aircraft. MacArthur had 277 aircraft of the U.S. Army Air Forces under his command in the Philippines. Only half the planes were first-line combat aircraft, including thirty-five early model B-17 four-engine bombers and about 54 P-40 Warhawk fighters.

In preparation for their assault on the Philippines, the Japanese had amassed a force of more than 800 aircraft. On the morning of December 8, 1941—just one day after the attack on Pearl Harbor—the Japanese sent 108 bombers and eighty-four Zero fighter escorts toward the Philippines. Their target was Clark Field on Luzon—the largest American military airfield in the Philippines. When the Japanese bombers and fighters arrived over Clark Field on December 8, almost all of MacArthur's planes were lined up in neat rows on the airfield, as they had been at Pearl Harbor. The Japanese pilots quickly destroyed the bulk of MacArthur's air support with minimal effort. Japanese losses for the day totaled only nine planes.

LEFT: U.S. Marines slog through deep mud along a jungle trail. Tropical jungles, in the broad sense, include rain forests, swamps, and batches of *kunai* grass. This was the type of terrain in which many American ground operations in the Pacific were fought during World War II.

The Japanese Type 95 HA-GO light tank first entered service in 1935. It was among the more common Japanese armored fighting vehicles encountered by American troops fighting in the Pacific during World War II. This tank was powered by a diesel engine that gave it a top speed of 28 miles per hour (45kph). The vehicle had a three-man crew and was armed with a turret-mounted 37-mm gun and, in later models, up to two machine guns.

Simultaneous with the attack on Clark Field, the Japanese attacked Nelson Field, also situated on Luzon, destroying even more U.S. planes. The Japanese also demolished a radar station and a number of American military barracks and warehouses on the island. On December 9, the Japanese attacked Nichols Field, near the Philippine capital of Manila, and took out yet another complement of MacArthur's planes. On December 10, Japanese aircraft attacked and destroyed the major American naval yard on Luzon. Fortunately, most of the American naval vessels had left the Philippines on the evening of December 8.

To the delight of the Japanese and to the utter shock of the United States' senior military and political leaders, in only two days' time MacArthur had lost almost all his air support at almost no cost to the enemy. While the senior U.S. Army and U.S. Navy commanders at Pearl Harbor were quickly relieved of command for being caught unprepared, MacArthur was never forced to answer for the catastrophe that befell his air-support assets. Despite calls for MacArthur's removal from command, Roosevelt and his top military advisors decided to leave him in charge of the defense of the Philippines, fearing that the American public, still reeling from the shock of the attack on Pearl Harbor, would be disheartened by the public ouster of their best-known general at such a key moment.

## The Japanese Landings Begin

Determined to press their advantage, small units of the Japanese Army began landing on various islands of the Philippines as early as December 8. The main Japanese invasion force of 43,000 men landed on Luzon two weeks later at Lingayen Gulf—about 100 miles (160km) from Manila. The invasion force included artillery units and more than 100 tanks. A secondary Japanese landing was made the next day, 200 miles (320km) southeast of Lingayen Bay. The Japanese objective was to attack Manila from both the north and the south, trapping MacArthur's forces in the middle.

MacArthur was in command of a Philippine Army of ten divisions plus support troops totaling approximately 100,000 men. Unfortunately, not a single Philippine Army division was up to full strength before the Japanese attack. None of these divisions had antitank weapons, and the shortage of artillery guns meant that they would not have the firepower support they needed to face the Japanese invaders on even terms.

The Philippine Army was backed up by a small American military contingent of about 25,000 soldiers, most of them stationed on Luzon. These troops were broken down as follows: 7,329 were assigned to infantry units. Another 4,967 men were assigned to the coastal artillery guns that protected Manila Bay and Subic Bay from Japanese naval attacks. The remaining troops served in support roles.

Despite the many shortcomings of the forces under his command, MacArthur remained confident that the Philippine Army could stop any landing attempts by the Japanese Army on Luzon. MacArthur's confidence soon evaporated, however, when Japanese units overwhelmed his troops and forced them to withdraw.

Soldiers of the Japanese Army storm ashore on a Pacific island during World War II. Japanese tactical doctrine always stressed the inherent superiority of offensive operations. This doctrine served them well during the fighting in China against poorly armed and poorly motivated opponents. By 1943 the overwhelming American advantage in firepower had rendered the Japanese Army doctrine dangerously obsolete.

RIGHT: The only major American military outpost (other than Pearl Harbor) that stood in the way of the Japanese conquest of east and southwest Asia was in the Philippines, about 5,000 miles (8,045km) from San Francisco. The bad news for the American military personnel on Luzon in December 1941 was the fact that Tokyo was less than 2,000 (3,200km) miles away.

OPPOSITE, TOP: A grim-faced MacArthur, accompanied by some of his staff, visits American and Philippine defensive positions on Bataan in early 1942. Only 25 miles (40km) long and 20 miles (32km) wide, the Bataan Peninsula juts out from the mainland of Luzon. Because MacArthur was convinced that he could defeat the Japanese invasion forces as they made their landings on the local beaches, he did not authorize the buildup of supplies on the Bataan Peninsula. When MacArthur's plans proved insufficient and his troops were forced back to Bataan, they suffered a great deal for want of a fully stocked supply base.

OPPOSITE, BOTTOM: Japanese soldiers employ the Type 93 flamethrower on an enemy defensive position. The weapon had a maximum range of 25 to 30 yards (23–27m) and could fire in continuous bursts of ten to twelve seconds. Flamethrowers were first used during World War I, and they aroused much fear and horror among soldiers of all armies.

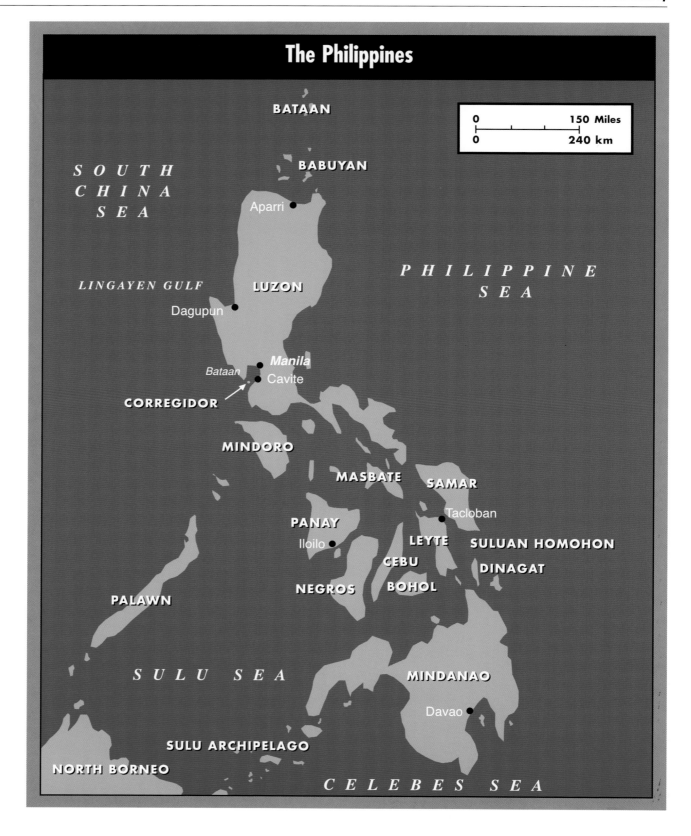

### The Philippines

0    150 Miles
0    240 km

BATAAN

BABUYAN

SOUTH CHINA SEA

Aparri

PHILIPPINE SEA

LINGAYEN GULF    LUZON

Dagupun

Manila

Bataan   Cavite

CORREGIDOR

MINDORO

MASBATE    SAMAR

Tacloban

PANAY    LEYTE    SULUAN HOMOHON

Iloilo    CEBU    DINAGAT

NEGROS   BOHOL

PALAWN

SULU SEA    MINDANAO

Davao

SULU ARCHIPELAGO

NORTH BORNEO

CELEBES SEA

# The Retreat Begins

Faced with an unstoppable Japanese ground offensive, MacArthur quickly called for a troop withdrawal into Luzon's mountainous Bataan Peninsula. This required an extremely complicated retrograde movement. Despite facing constant enemy attack, MacArthur and his commanders completed the withdrawal by January 7, 1942.

During the withdrawal to Bataan, almost 12,000 of MacArthur's remaining Philippine Army soldiers deserted their units rather than continue what they believed was a futile fight. Even worse, not enough food had been sent to Bataan before the withdrawal began, and as a result the troops were soon facing severe food shortages.

By January 2, 1942, the Japanese had occupied Manila, which had been declared an open city (a city that would not be defended) on December 24, 1941. MacArthur's Luzon force was practically intact, but it was trapped in Bataan, on the island of Corregidor, and on three small islands in Manila Bay. MacArthur had moved his staff and family to Corregidor on December 24, 1941. On the night of March 11, 1942, MacArthur left Corregidor for Australia under orders from President Roosevelt. He arrived in Australia on March 17, 1942.

The starving American soldiers left behind on Bataan saw little or no glory in fighting a hopeless delaying action against the Japanese. They made up a song that did much to explain their feelings at the time:

*We're the battling bastards of Bataan;*
*No mama, no papa, no Uncle Sam;*
*No aunts, no uncles, no cousins, no nieces;*
*No pills, no planes, no artillery pieces . . .*
*And nobody gives a damn.*

American and Philippine troops were not aware that America's senior leaders had abandoned their plans to defend the Philippines. With the U.S. Navy Pacific Fleet in shambles and an unprotected supply line stretching more than 5,000 miles (8,045km) from the Philippines to the West Coast of the United States, there was little that could be done. Even if there had been additional U.S. Army units available for the relief

Dejected American and Philippine soldiers on Bataan await orders from their Japanese captors. Major General Edward P. King Jr. surrendered his 78,000 troops in Bataan to the Japanese on April 9, 1942. Some wanted to fight on, but with supplies exhausted and thousands of wounded and sick in the area, plus 40,000 civilian refugees to worry about, he feared further resistance would result only in unnecessary loss of life. Unfortunately, the ensuing march of prisoners of war to the camp near Cabanatuan was brutal in the extreme.

of the Philippines, there were not enough troop transport ships in early 1942.

Facing overwhelming odds and under constant attack, the American and Philippine troops on Bataan held on for roughly two months after MacArthur left for Australia. Finally, on April 9, 1942, after these troops were reduced to the point of military helplessness by hunger, disease, and casualties, Major General Edward P. King, Jr., their commanding officer, decided that he had no choice but to surrender.

On May 5, 1942, the Japanese managed to land troops on Corregidor. Despite heavy losses, the invaders continued to funnel more troops and tanks onto the island. On May 6, Lieutenant General Jonathan M. Wainwright, MacArthur's successor in the Philippines, surrendered the remainder of the American and Philippine forces to the local Japanese military commanders. Forced by the Japanese to take the infamous "Bataan Death March" to prison camp, thousands of the already weakened American and Phillippine soldiers perished.

# Regrouping for the Next Round

On May 8, 1942, two days after the surrender of the Philippines, MacArthur sent President Roosevelt a message, describing his opinion of the threat now posed to Australia by the Japanese military. An extract from that message reads:

> *I deem it of the utmost importance to provide adequate security for Australia and the Pacific Area, thus maintaining a constant frontal defense and a flank threat against further movement to the southward. This should be followed at the earliest possible moment by offensive action or at least by a sufficiently dangerous initial threat of offensive action to affect the enemy plans and dispositions.*

Implementation of these two initiatives would enable MacArthur to build up a strong base of operations in Australia and to defend the line of communications between the United States and Australia. This was critically important, for Australia was the last base of

## P-40 Warhawk

**The most common fighter in the inventory of the U.S. Army Air Force in the opening stages of World War II was the P-40 Warhawk built by the Curtiss-Wright Airplane Division in Buffalo, New York.**

**The P-40B model of the Warhawk flown at Pearl Harbor and in the Philippines was powered by a liquid-cooled, V-12 Allison piston engine that produced 1,150 horsepower and gave it a top speed of 352 mph (566kph) at 15,000 feet (4,745m). It could climb to that height in 5.1 minutes. The maximum ceiling of the P-40B was 32,400 feet (11,275m). Operational range was 240 miles (386km). Armament consisted of two .50-caliber and two .30-caliber Browning air-cooled machine guns.**

**The P-40 Warhawk was considered obsolete when compared to better-performing Japanese aircraft it encountered in the first year of the war in the Pacific. Nevertheless, it held the line against superior Japanese aircraft in the Pacific until replaced in early 1943 by the Lockheed twin-engine P-38 Lightning long-range fighter.**

More than 14,000 P-40 Warhawk fighters were built in various versions by American aircraft manufacturers during World War II. The two aircraft seen here are examples of the F-model of the P-40, which was powered by a Packard-built copy of a British Rolls-Royce Merlin engine.

# Eastern New Guinea and the Bismarck Archipelago

ADMIRALTY ISLANDS

Hollandia

Wewak

*BISMARCK SEA*

BISMARCK ARCHIPELAGO

**NEW IRELAND**

Rabaul

*VITIAZ STRAIT*

*DAMPIER STRAIT*

**NEW GUINEA**

**NEW BRITAIN**

Finschhafen

Lae

*Bougainville*

Gasmata

Salamaua

Wau

*HUON GULF*

*HOLNICOTE BAY*

*SOLOMON SEA*

CAPE WARD HUNT

Gona

Kokoda

Sananada

Buna

Tufi

*GULF OF PAPUA*

Port Moresby

*Trobriand Islands*

*Goodenough*

*Fergusson*

*D'Entrecasteaux Islands*

Rabi

*MILNE BAY*

**PAPUAN PENINSULA**

**AUSTRALIA**

*CORAL SEA*

*LOUISIADE ARCHIPELAGO*

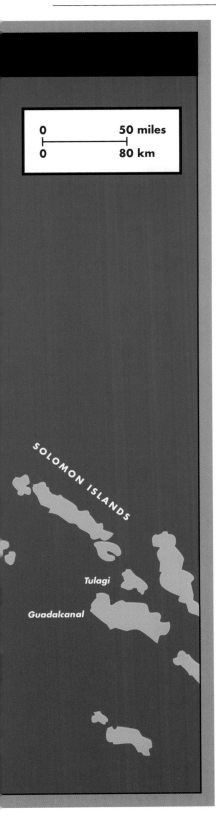

LEFT: The large Japanese military base at Rabaul, on the eastern tip of New Britain Island in the center of the Bismarck Archipelago, posed a double threat to the Americans and Australians from 1942 through the early months of 1944. Home base for many Japanese warships and planes, it menaced the line of communication from the United States to Australia, and it blocked any Allied advance along the north coast of New Guinea to the Philippines. The elimination of Rabaul therefore became the primary mission of the Allied forces of the south and southwest Pacific areas during this period. Executing this mission, code-named "Cartwheel," these forces fought a long series of ground, air, and naval battles across the vast region shown on the map.

operations left to the Allies in the Southwest Pacific after the fall of the Philippines.

By March 1942, the Japanese had taken the British fortress of Singapore and had overrun the oil-rich Dutch East Indies. They were also beginning to threaten the supply line between the United States and Australia. The Japanese drive into the Solomon Islands and Port Moresby in New Guinea threatened Australia itself.

America's senior military leaders amassed every unit they had available to strengthen the 6,000-mile (9,642km) line to Australia. Air bases were garrisoned along a string of islands from Hawaii to New Zealand so that the Army Air Forces could help the Navy keep the line open.

By prior agreement with the British government, the Pacific Theater was made an area of U.S. strategic responsibility in the spring of 1942. Once the British had agreed that the Pacific Theater should be an American responsibility, the Joint Chiefs of Staff divided the theater into two major areas: the Southwest Pacific Area (the SWPA) and the Pacific Ocean Areas (POA). MacArthur was named supreme commander of the SWPA, which included Australia, New Guinea, the Philippine Islands, the South China Sea, the Gulf of

ABOVE: Japanese soldiers give a cheer in this posed picture taken shortly after their capture of the American-held island of Corregidor. The small island was located in the middle of Manila Bay. In the background is a large American 12-inch (30cm) coastal artillery gun used unsuccessfully to defend the island. Besides the massive 12-inch guns, there were also a number of 6-inch (15cm), 10-inch (25cm), and 14-inch (35cm) coastal artillery guns installed on Corregidor and on the other islands guarding Manila Bay.

Siam, and the Netherlands East Indies (except Sumatra). Admiral Chester W. Nimitz, who was already commanding the U.S. Navy Pacific Fleet, was named the commander in chief of the Pacific Ocean Areas. The Navy further subdivided the POA into three subordinate commands: the North, Central, and South Pacific areas. Nimitz commanded the North and Central Pacific areas directly. Vice Admiral Robert L. Ghormley was placed in command of the South Pacific area.

President Roosevelt and General George C. Marshall, head of the Joint Chiefs, believed that a single supreme commander in charge of all naval, ground, and air units should be appointed in the Pacific Theater. Unfortunately, the Army and the Navy each refused to serve under the command of the other service. This fierce interservice rivalry led to each getting its own theater of operations. Instead of a single major advance toward Japan, there would be two separate advances—one through the Central Pacific and the other through the Southwest Pacific.

ABOVE: President Franklin D. Roosevelt had hoped to name a single U.S. commander to oversee all military operations in the Pacific, as he had done in Europe. This plan, however, ran afoul of strong Army-Navy interservice rivalries. Neither would consent to serve under an officer of the rival service. Seen here on the deck of a warship is Roosevelt, flanked by MacArthur (left) and Admiral Chester W. Nimitz.
RIGHT: The harbor of Rabaul, on the northeastern tip of the Japanese-controlled island of New Britain, on November 11, 1943, seen from an American military aircraft. Stationed all around are Japanese warships, some of them steaming out of the harbor in fear of an American aerial attack.

The Joint Chiefs preferred the Central Pacific route for the main effort. It was a shorter route to the Japanese home islands and would require fewer ships, men, and supplies. It would also allow for the destruction of the Japanese Fleet as it assembled to oppose the American advance. In the SWPA, a drive from New Guinea to the Philippines would face a number of large Japanese-occupied islands in the same general area that could provide mutual support for each other. In the Central Pacific, the Japanese-occupied islands were small and too spread out for mutual support, and therefore vulnerable to the continuously expanding U.S. Navy Pacific Fleet.

## Choosing Objectives

In the early summer of 1942, it became possible for the United States, Australia, and New Zealand to launch a limited offensive to protect the Allied line of communications and to prevent the Japanese from consolidating their gains. On July 2, 1942, the Joint Chiefs of Staff issued orders that set in motion the first offensive of the Pacific war. Rabaul, located on the island of New Britain in the Bismarck Archipelago, was the target. With its large harbor, numerous airfields, and excellent natural defenses, Rabaul was the strategic hub of the Japanese defenses in the Southwest Pacific. Rabaul provided a sanctuary for the Japanese, a place where they could resupply their forces in the Solomon Islands, launch an assault on Australia, or threaten the vital supply lines linking Australia and America.

Capturing Rabaul was far beyond the capabilities of the meager forces available to the Allies in July 1942. Therefore, the Joint Chiefs specified that it would be taken in three stages. The first stage would be the seizure of bases in the southern Solomons. The second would consist of the reoccupation of the remainder of the Solomons and the north coast of New Guinea as far as Lae and Salamaua. The third stage would be the recapture of Rabaul itself, along with the rest of the Bismarck Archipelago.

In laying the groundwork for the projected offensive in July, the Joint Chiefs gave the command of the South

Pacific Area (and control over the first stage of the offensive against Rabaul) to Vice Admiral Robert L. Ghormley. Ghormley would, in turn, be subordinate to Admiral Nimitz, who commanded the North and Central Pacific Areas. In his own area, Ghormley exercised unity of command over all the forces at his disposal—sea, ground, and air.

The Joint Chiefs assigned strategic direction of the second and final phases of the offensive against Rabaul to MacArthur and Nimitz. The Joint Chiefs decided to reserve for themselves control over the assignment of tasks, the allocation of resources, and the timing of operations in the two areas. This would provide them with the final word if disagreements arose between MacArthur and his naval counterparts. As the war continued, the disagreements between MacArthur and the Navy about the direction of the war in the Pacific increased, eventually becoming so heated that President Roosevelt himself frequently had to step into the fray to make the final decisions.

An M4 Sherman medium tank of the 1st Marine Corps Division drives off a U.S. Navy Landing Ship, Tank (LST) onto the beach at Cape Gloucester on December 26, 1943. Cape Gloucester was located on the western tip of the island of New Britain. With its seizure, MacArthur could protect the waterway through which his ships would have to pass on the way to the Philippines. It took the Marines three weeks of hard and bloody fighting to take the area away from the Japanese Army.

The crew of a Marine Corps 75-mm Pack Howitzer on Guadalcanal prepares to load their weapon prior to firing on Japanese positions. The weapon saw extensive service with the Marine Corps throughout World War II; it was used in almost every major amphibious landing in the Pacific. Operated by a five-man crew, the small howitzer could hurl a 16-pound (7.3kg) high-explosive shell a maximum of 10,000 yards (9,120m).

# The Battle for Guadalcanal

Despite MacArthur's insistence that the taking of Rabual be the first goal in the Southwest Pacific, the Joint Chiefs instituted a different plan. The first American offensive operation against the Japanese outer defensive perimeter began on August 7, 1942, with the landing of a Marine division on a sleepy island at the southern end of the Solomon Island chain—Guadalcanal.

The Japanese Army, deeply involved in the conquest of Southeast Asia, expressed little concern over the American presence in the Solomons. When the proper resources could be spared from more important areas, the Japanese Army planned to dispose quickly of the American forces on Guadalcanal.

The Japanese Navy, however, took the opposite approach and reacted vigorously to the American landing. Beginning on August 8, there began a series of bloody sea and air battles in the Solomons that would last for more than three months. The result was the destruction of Japanese air power in the area and the withdrawal of all major Japanese naval units. Once this occurred, the Japanese ground forces on Guadalcanal were doomed, despite heavy reinforcements that had arrived in the preceding months.

An example of the fierce fighting on Guadalcanal in the first months can be found in this extract from the Medal of Honor citation of Marine Sergeant Mitchell Paige for an action that occurred on October 26, 1942:

*When the enemy broke through the line directly in front of his position, Platoon Sergeant Paige, commanding a machine-gun section with fearless determination, continued to direct the fire of his gunners until all his men were either killed or wounded. Alone, against the deadly hail of Japanese shells, he fought his gun and when it was destroyed, took another, moving from gun to gun, never ceasing his withering fire against the advancing hordes until reinforcements finally arrived. Then, forming a new line, he dauntlessly and aggressively led a bayonet charge, driving the enemy back and preventing a break-through in our lines.*

By January 1943, fresh Marine and Army divisions were pushing the sick and starving Japanese ground troops into a corner of Guadalcanal. To save their remaining troops, the Japanese Navy implemented a secret nighttime evacuation of more than 10,000 troops during the first week of February 1943. Despite this set-back, the successful conquest of Guadalcanal provided the Allies with their first large-scale victory over the Empire of Japan.

Once the Japanese were driven out of Guadalcanal, American forces quickly began to construct major air and logistical bases in preparation for further advances in the region. Now that the Allies were firmly established in the Solomon Islands, the drive to encircle Rabaul could begin.

## The Fighting Continues

In August 1942, the Japanese had begun pushing over-land, across the towering Owen Stanley Mountains of New Guinea toward Port Moresby, from the northeastern coast of the island. By mid-September, they were within 20 miles (32 km) of their objective. MacArthur now had to commit strong Australian units to push the Japanese back to the north coast in an operation known as the Papuan Campaign.

By the middle of November, the Japanese were firmly entrenched in the Buna-Gona region of New

Guinea. Here, as at Guadalcanal, they received reinforcements from the nearby stronghold of Rabaul. The Japanese clung desperately to their positions in New Guinea. It took almost three months and the combined efforts of two Australian divisions and a single American division to clear the Japanese from the Buna-Gona area of New Guinea.

In March 1943, the Japanese made a major effort to reinforce their position in New Guinea by sending a large convoy to the island. The ensuing battle, called the Battle of the Bismarck Sea, resulted in the loss of more than 3,500 men and many valuable ships. During the following month, Japanese aircraft from Rabaul and Truk (a Japanese stronghold in the Caroline Islands) sought unsuccessfully to knock out Allied air power in the Solomons. The Japanese lost a significant number of carrier planes and pilots in this battle, which further reduced the capabilities of the Japanese Navy. They also lost their commander. Admiral Yamamoto was shot down over Bougainville (the largest island in the Solomons) in an aerial ambush.

During the five-month lull that followed the campaigns in Papua and Guadalcanal, Admiral Halsey

Looking down the wrong end of two .50-caliber machine guns mounted on a U.S. Navy PT Boat somewhere in the Pacific Ocean during World War II. The typical wartime PT Boat had two sets of twin .50-caliber machine guns installed in manually operated open-topped turrets. The .50-caliber machine gun was an excellent anti-aircraft, antipersonnel, and antiship weapon (though it was effective only against unarmored vessels).

# The Japanese Zero

**One of the biggest advantages enjoyed by the Japanese Imperial Navy in the first months of the war in the Pacific was that offered by its carrier-based fighter, the Mitsubishi Zeke, more popularly known as the "Zero." It possessed exceptional range and maneuverability and proved superior to American land- and carrier-based fighters in 1941 and 1942.**

**A Nakajima NK2F Sakae 21 air-cooled radial piston engine gave the first production model of the Zero a top speed of 351 mph (565kph) at a height of 19,685 feet (6,000m). The Zero could climb to a ceiling of 19,685 feet (6,000m) in 7 minutes. With an extra fuel tank carried under the plane's fuselage, the Zero had a maximum operational range of 710 miles (1,142km).**

**Armament on the Zero consisted of a 7.7-mm and a 13.2-mm machine gun in the nose of the aircraft, as well as two wing-mounted 20-mm automatic cannons. It could also carry two 132-pound (60kg) bombs or a single 551-pound (250kg) bomb.**

**With the appearance of more advanced American aircraft in early 1943, such as the carrier-based U.S. Navy Grumman F6F Hellcat, the Zero lost the edge that it once had and became a liability instead of an asset to the Japanese Navy.**

A Japanese Navy Mitsubishi A6M fighter, better known to Americans as the "Zero," taking off from an aircraft carrier flight deck. The Zero was the first fighter designed for naval use that outperformed its land-based counterparts.

(who had been promoted to commander of the South Pacific Area) and General MacArthur gathered their resources and prepared bases for the second phase of the drive toward Rabaul, which began in late June 1943 with landings by MacArthur's forces on islands off eastern New Guinea and on the New Guinea coast northwest of Buna.

In August 1943, Admiral Halsey's South Pacific forces, now operating under MacArthur's strategic direction, landed on New Georgia Island, northwest of Guadalcanal in the Solomons. As Halsey's forces were landing, the Joint Chiefs, with President Roosevelt and Prime Minister Winston Churchill's approval, changed their minds about the necessity of a direct assault on Rabaul. Their alternative plan was to continue to surround Rabaul and then allow Allied air and naval units to neutralize its offensive capabilities. To defend Rabaul from aerial attack, the Japanese deployed 367 anti-aircraft guns in and around the base; these guns provided little help.

During October 1943, New Zealander troops and U.S. Marines continued their northwestern advance up the Solomon Island chain by landing on the islands of Treasury and Choiseul. These small islands served as secure bases for the assault on the large island of Bougainville, which held a Japanese garrison of almost 50,000 men.

The invasion of Bougainville began on November 1, 1943, when Marine and Army divisions landed. The subsequent series of fierce battles lasted until March 1944. These bloody engagements broke the back of Japanese resistance on the island. The remaining Japanese personnel, lacking any outside source of supplies, were hunted down by Australian troops in the following months. With the taking of Bougainville and its airfields, the main part of the South Pacific Area's task—surrounding Rabaul—was finished.

On December 15, 1943, MacArthur commenced a new series of operations with the objective of completing the encirclement of Rabaul. U.S. Army units landed on the western side of New Britain Island (Rabaul was located across the island, on the eastern side). On December 26, a Marine Division landed on the north coast of New Britain. In mid-February 1944, New

The U.S. Navy cruiser *Quincy* seen from a nearby ship shortly before the invasion of Guadalcanal. The *Quincy* was sunk a few days later during one of the numerous naval battles that raged around the island of Guadalcanal between August 7, 1942, and February 7, 1943. In this conflict, each side lost twenty-four warships. Because of America's impressive industrial capability, the U.S. Navy was able to replace lost ships. The Japanese, however, were not. In the grand war of attrition that would be waged between the two navies, the Japanese could not keep up; they were doomed to lose in the long run.

Zealander troops of the South Pacific Area secured an air base site on Green Island (north of New Britain). On the last day of February, MacArthur began landing the U.S. Army's First Cavalry Division on the Admiralty Islands (located northwest of New Britain Island), effectively cutting off the western and north-western approaches to Rabaul.

Marines under Halsey seized an air base site on Emirau, north of Rabaul, on March 20, 1944, while Marine and Army units under MacArthur secured additional positions in western and central New Britain between March and May 1944, resulting in the complete encirclement of Rabaul.

By the end of the war, the Allies had dropped a total of 20,584 tons (18,526 metric tons) of bombs on Rabaul and had fired 383 tons (347,764kg) of naval shells at the Japanese base. At Rabaul, the Japanese lost the best of their flight personnel and suffered the damage or loss of 53 warships, 154 large cargo vessels, and 517 barges. The Japanese garrison of 98,000 troops at Rabaul sat out the rest of the war waiting for an invasion fleet that never arrived.

# Chapter 3

# Sea Battles in the Pacific

ON THE SAME DAY THAT THE JAPANESE BEGAN THEIR ATTACK ON THE PHILIPPINES, they set into motion plans to capture the American-occupied island of Guam (part of the Mariana chain of islands in the Central Pacific). With fewer than 200 Marines to defend the large, 228-square-mile (367-square-km) island, it quickly fell to a Japanese landing force of 5,500 men on December 10, 1941.

Another target of the Japanese war machine in the Central Pacific was the tiny American-occupied atoll of Wake. Unlike the American force in Guam, the Marine Corps garrison of 552 men on Wake put up a very tough fight. The outnumbered Marines lasted from December 8 to December 23. This small force was responsible for the loss of two Japanese ships, twenty-one aircraft, and 1,175 men.

After the crippling of the American Pacific Fleet at Pearl Harbor, the only other American naval force in the Pacific during the early months of 1942 was the small Asiatic Fleet in the Southwest Pacific. It included three cruisers, thirteen aging destroyers, and twenty-nine submarines. With this force, the U.S. Navy undertook to delay Japan's offensive operations in that area of the world until sufficient strength could be mustered to put up real resistance. This was a dangerous assignment, and the Asiatic Fleet was doomed from the start. Its dying gasp was the Battle of

LEFT: On December 15, 1942, two torpedoes from a Japanese submarine struck the U.S. Navy aircraft carrier *Wasp*, rupturing the ship's aviation fuel lines as well as its water mains, crippling the crew's ability to fight fires. Once the ship caught on fire, it was a lost cause, and within thirty minutes the *Wasp* was abandoned and sinking.

One of four Japanese Navy Myoko Class heavy cruisers before World War II. The main armament of these powerful warships consisted of ten 8-inch (20cm) guns arranged in five twin-gun armored turrets. The Myoko cruisers also had up to sixteen torpedo tubes and a number of smaller-caliber anti-aircraft guns.

the Java Sea on February 27, 1942. During that engagement, an Allied naval force made up of American, Dutch, and British units on five cruisers and ten destroyers attempted to intercept a Japanese invasion convoy protected by three cruisers and eighteen destroyers that was heading toward Java (the Dutch East Indies). The Allied ships, under the overall command of Dutch Rear Admiral Karel Doorman, were routed and suffered heavy losses.

The Japanese depended primarily on their land-based air power to advance through the Philippine Islands and the Dutch East Indies. After building up their strength at a given land base, they would overwhelm the consistently inferior Allied air opposition at the next point of attack and then send along heavily defended amphibious forces to make landings. As a rule, the distances were too short to permit attack by the remaining American naval forces in the area while the enemy was en route. As soon as the Japanese were in control of a new area, they would repair the airfields and gather forces for the next attack. These tactics were well suited to the geography of the Philippine Islands and the Dutch East Indies.

LEFT: The Japanese Navy employed the twin-engine Mitsubishi G3M, which entered production in 1937, in a variety of roles, including medium bomber, torpedo bomber, and long-range maritime patrol plane. American military personnel referred to it as the "Nell." BELOW LEFT: The oldest light cruisers in the U.S. Navy to serve during World War II were the ten ships of the Omaha Class, which entered service between 1923 and 1925. They were originally designed as fast scouting vessels armed with up to twelve 6-inch (15cm) guns. During World War II, the number of small-caliber antiaircraft guns on the ships was doubled to protect them from aerial attack. The Omaha Class light cruisers had a range of over 10,000 miles (16,000km) at 15 knots, or 3,000 miles (4,800km) at 30 knots.

Admiral Chester W. Nimitz graduated as an ensign from the U.S. Navy Academy at Annapolis in 1905. He quickly rose through the ranks. Shortly after the Japanese attack on Pearl Harbor, he was appointed commander-in-chief of the American Pacific Fleet, a position he retained till the end of the war.

## The First American Offensive Operations

By January 1942, the situation in the Southwest Pacific and Southeast Asia was growing steadily worse, as the Japanese continued offensive operations after the attack on Pearl Harbor. Admiral Chester A. Nimitz, commander of the U.S. Navy Pacific Fleet, had little choice but to strike back at the Japanese. His first targets were the Marshall and Gilbert islands—by then occupied by the Japanese and comprising a part of the Japanese outer perimeter defensive line.

Admiral William F. Halsey, Jr., volunteered to carry out the raids beginning on February 1, 1942, with a force consisting of two carriers, five cruisers, and ten destroyers. The operation was a success. Except for one cruiser, which suffered a single bomb hit, and the carrier *Enterprise*, which was slightly damaged by shell fragments, none of the U.S. Navy vessels was damaged during the entire operation. Personnel losses and injuries were similarly slight.

Halsey's successful pattern was followed by several other operations conducted during the following weeks.

Flight deck personnel prepare a squadron of Grumman F4F "Wildcat" fighters for launching from the wooden flight deck of a U.S. Navy aircraft carrier early in World War II. The Wildcat first entered Navy service in 1940. It remained the Navy's first-line carrier fighter until, beginning in early 1943, it was superseded by the much-improved Grumman F6F "Hellcat" fighter.

Crew members listen to a briefing by a senior officer on the wooden flight deck of a Japanese Navy aircraft carrier during World War II. The mattresslike devices attached to the bridge of the ship provide a small measure of extra protection from ammunition fragments. In the foreground is a Mitsubishi A6M Zeke, or "Zero," ready for launching.

On February 20, 1942, a task force built around the carrier *Lexington*, which was commanded by Vice Admiral Wilson Brown, attempted a combination air and ground attack on the massive Japanese Army and Navy base at Rabaul, New Britain. During its approach, the *Lexington* was discovered by a formation of Japanese twin-engine bombers, sixteen of which were destroyed by American planes and ship-mounted anti-aircraft guns. The element of surprise having been lost and fuel having been reduced by high-speed maneuvering, the attack on Rabaul was canceled.

On February 24, 1942, Admiral Halsey shelled and bombed Wake Island using the carrier *Enterprise*, two cruisers, and seven destroyers. Wake had been in Japanese hands since December 23, 1941. Eight days later, planes from the *Enterprise* bombed Marcus Island with reasonably satisfactory results. Only one plane was lost in the operation.

On March 10, Vice Admiral Wilson Brown, with the carriers *Lexington* and *Yorktown* and supporting ships, raided the New Guinea ports of Salamaua and Lae, where Japanese troops had landed three days earlier. A number of enemy warships and transport vessels were sunk or damaged with only light losses among U.S. Navy planes.

The loss of Japanese transport ships in this battle

Lieutenant Colonel James H. Doolittle (standing, left) addresses his men on the flight deck of the U.S. Navy aircraft carrier *Hornet* shortly before their bold attack on the Japanese home islands launched on April 18, 1942. Doolittle first became a pilot in the U.S. Army during World War I. In the years between the two world wars, he amassed considerable fame as a civilian air-racing pilot. In 1940 Doolittle returned to service in the Army as a major in charge of organizing aircraft production in former civilian automobile factories.

\* England yanked most Australia's military to the Mediterranean to fight the nazis, leaving Australia virtually defenseless. The American effort at New Guinea ended the threat of invasion for Australia. A result of this history was that the Australians became big fans of the U.S. and had bitter feelings toward the crown. JL

delayed Japan's plans for an attack on Port Moresby—an important Australian military base on the southwestern tip of New Guinea—for over two months. Japanese control over Port Moresby would have posed a direct air attack threat to northern Australia and would have made a Japanese invasion of Australia feasible. \*

On April 18, the U.S. Navy carrier *Hornet* successfully launched sixteen U.S. Army twin-engine B-25 bombers on a one-way mission to bomb the Japanese capital of Tokyo and other targets. This operation is commonly referred to as the Doolittle Raid, after its commander, Lieutenant Colonel James H. Doolittle, a famous prewar civilian racing pilot.

The original plans for the Doolittle Raid had called for the flight crews to pilot their aircraft to friendly Chinese airfields after bombing Japan. However, all the U.S. Army bombers ran out of fuel before reaching safety in China and crashed after their flight crews bailed out. Of the eighty pilots and flight crewmen to take part in the raid, seventy-one survived—including Doolittle. One was killed in his parachute descent. The Japanese captured eight Americans from the raid and executed three of them. Another American died in captivity.

The Doolittle Raid was suggested by President Roosevelt, who sought to raise the morale of the American public by striking at the very heart of the Japanese Empire in a surprise attack. While the material damage to the Japanese homeland was slight, the Japanese military's humiliation was acute and resulted in an immediate acceleration of their offensive operations and the strengthening of their defenses in the Pacific.

To help prevent another Doolittle-type raid on Japan, the Japanese military decided to capture the small American-occupied atoll of Midway, located 1,110 miles (1,786km) west of Hawaii. By this action, the Japanese Navy also hoped to draw out and engage the U.S. Navy Pacific Fleet's carriers in a major, decisive battle.

As the Japanese Navy began making plans to bring its warships together for the attack on the island of Midway, another major sea battle was brewing in the Southwest Pacific that would greatly affect Japanese plans for the Battle of Midway.

## The Battle of the Coral Sea

From encrypted Japanese radio transmissions intercepted and deciphered in April 1942, the U.S. Navy was aware of Japanese plans to seize Port Moresby on May 10. The invasion force was to consist of twelve troop transport ships escorted by several destroyers, four cruisers, and three aircraft carriers.

The Americans were also able to track the Japanese invasion force by monitoring the location and volume of radio transmissions from Japanese warships. Employing this method, called radio traffic analysis, American naval analysts could predict Japanese ship movements with a fair degree of accuracy.

In addition to Port Moresby, the Japanese planned to occupy Tulagi, a small island in the southern Solomons. From this location, Japanese planes would be able to stop American scout planes from entering the eastern approaches to the Coral Sea to look for enemy ships.

It should be noted that during the first five months of the war in the Pacific, nearly every naval engagement with the Japanese had demonstrated the importance of air power. Japanese superiority in the air was a major factor in American losses in the Pacific early in the war. Similarly, the successful but inconclusive American carrier raids on the Japanese-held islands in the Pacific had inspired confidence within the senior leadership of the U.S. Navy because the costs had been so low. The unknown for both sides was the potential outcome of a direct battle between opposing carrier forces.

OPPOSITE: Taken on board the U.S. Navy aircraft carrier *Yorktown* during the Battle of the Coral Sea in May 1942, this photograph shows a variety of anti-aircraft guns mounted along one side of the ship's wooden flight deck. The single-barrel weapons in the foreground and background are 20-mm Oerlikon automatic guns. Protected by thin armored shields, the Oerlikons had a rate of fire of 450 rounds per minute and an effective range of 2,000 yards (1,828m). The four-barreled weapon located between the Oerlikons is a 1.1-inch (2.75cm) Navy-Hudson anti-aircraft gun. Each gun could fire up to 150 rounds per minute or all four guns could work together could pump out 600 rounds per minute. LEFT: U.S. Navy torpedo planes attack the Japanese Navy aircraft carrier *Shoho* during the Battle of the Coral Sea in May 1942. Two torpedo planes—one just below the center of the ship, the other above the stern (rear)—circle the already burning ship.

When the Japanese began to occupy Tulagi Island on May 3, 1942, Rear Admiral Frank J. Fletcher proceeded north from the Coral Sea to intercept the Japanese invasion fleet with a force composed of the carrier *Yorktown*, three cruisers, and six destroyers.

The next morning, in a series of heavy attacks, planes from the *Yorktown* sank a number of Japanese vessels anchored off Tulagi. The three Japanese carriers sent to protect the invasion fleet had been delayed and were unable to provide critical aerial protection. The remaining Japanese ships soon headed back to the safety of Rabaul.

On May 5, Rear Admiral Fletcher's force had joined other Allied naval units heading toward the Japanese

fleet destined for Port Moresby. Fletcher knew that the Japanese invasion force would have to transit the southeastern tip of New Guinea, so he stationed an attack group within striking distance of the probable path of the Japanese fleet. The remainder of his force moved northward in an attempt to locate enemy covering forces.

On the morning of May 7, Fletcher encountered the Japanese light carrier *Shoho*, which was quickly sunk by aircraft from the *Lexington* and the *Yorktown*. Only one American dive-bomber was lost during the attack. Soon afterward, the Japanese launched a massive strike at what they believed was the location of the two American carriers. Instead, they found only the U.S. Navy oil

ABOVE: Vice Admiral Frank J. Fletcher was in tactical command of U.S. Navy forces during the Battle of the Coral Sea in May 1942. A month later, he commanded one of the two American task forces to take part in the crucial Battle of Midway. Ships under his command also took part in the fighting around Guadalcanal. RIGHT: Smoke generated by a number of uncontrolled fires within the hull of the U.S. Navy aircraft carrier *Lexington* rises from the ship's flight deck. At least two torpedoes and two bombs struck the *Lexington* during the Battle of the Coral Sea in May 1942. Damaged beyond saving, the ship was abandoned by its crew and later sunk by five torpedoes from a U.S. Navy destroyer.

tanker *Neosho* and the destroyer *Sims*, both of which were promptly sunk.

The next morning, American planes made contact with the Japanese carriers *Shokadu* and *Zuikaku*, four heavy cruisers, and several destroyers. The *Shokadu* was attacked and slightly damaged, while the *Zuikaku* escaped with no damage under cover of bad weather. The Japanese carriers counterattacked about an hour later. The *Yorktown* and the *Lexington* were both damaged, the latter rather severely. Early in the afternoon of May 8, an explosion in the already damaged *Lexington* made it impossible to save and the ship was abandoned. Nearly all of her personnel were saved, however. A U.S. Navy destroyer sank the *Lexington* with torpedoes. The *Yorktown*, despite her battle damage, retreated under her own power.

Thus ended the first major engagement in naval history in which surface ships did not exchange a single shot between them. Although the loss of the *Lexington* was keenly felt, the engagement in the Coral Sea effectively checked the Japanese in their advance southward toward Australia. The battle also kept the Japanese carriers *Zuikaku* and *Shokadu* from participating in the Battle of Midway a few weeks later. Many naval historians believe that the carriers' presence at Midway could have turned the battle in favor of the Japanese.

## The Battle of Midway

After the Battle of the Coral Sea, the U.S. Navy intercepted Japanese plans for an attack on the island of Midway. To lay a trap for the Japanese fleet, U.S. Navy carriers and supporting vessels were recalled from the South Pacific Area. The aircraft carrier *Yorktown*, damaged only weeks earlier at the Battle of the Coral Sea, was rushed back into service after temporary repairs. Scouting and patrol lines were established well to the west of Midway for early detection of the advancing Japanese invasion force.

U.S. Navy forces consisted of the carriers *Enterprise*, *Hornet*, and *Yorktown*, their 233 planes, eight cruisers, fourteen destroyers, and about twenty submarines. These were divided into two task forces,

* The U.S. cracked the Japanese military code in 1939. They never caught on and never bothered to change it. So the U.S. always knew where they planned to attack. What about Pearl Harbor? Good question. — J.T.

# Aircraft Carriers

Aircraft carriers are basically mobile bases for planes capable of moving aircraft into striking distance of vast areas that were formerly inaccessible. During World War II, they were the most indispensable ships in the U.S. and Japanese navies. Without them, a naval fleet, no matter how impressive in size and strength, would be helpless to defend itself from massed aerial attack from an enemy's land- or carrier-based aircraft. It would be the American ability to build and staff aircraft carriers in large numbers that would doom the Japanese Navy.

BELOW: The original U.S. Navy aircraft carrier *Hornet* (designated CV-8) entered service in October 1941. It was one of three ships in the Yorktown Class; the other two were the *Yorktown*, sunk in June 1942, and the *Enterprise*, which survived the war badly damaged. The *Hornet* was sunk during the Battle of Santa Cruz Islands on October 26, 1942. In a longstanding tradition of honoring ships retired from service or lost in battle, the Navy bestowed the name *Hornet* upon a new aircraft carrier of the Essex Class, which entered service in November 1943. The new *Hornet* (designated CV-12) enjoyed a remarkable wartime career and took a heavy toll of Japanese ships and planes.

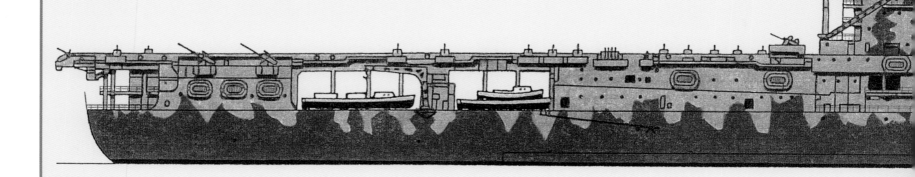

OPPOSITE: The motion of the Grumman F6F Hellcat's fast-moving propeller causes an "aura" to form as the plane is about to be launched off the flight deck of the U.S. Navy aircraft carrier *Yorktown*. The Hellcat was a greatly improved version of the earlier Grumman F4F Wildcat. LEFT: An impressive lineup of U.S. Navy warships steams toward its next objective somewhere in the Pacific during World War II. In the lead are two aircraft carriers, escorted by a number of battleships armed with anti-aircraft guns.

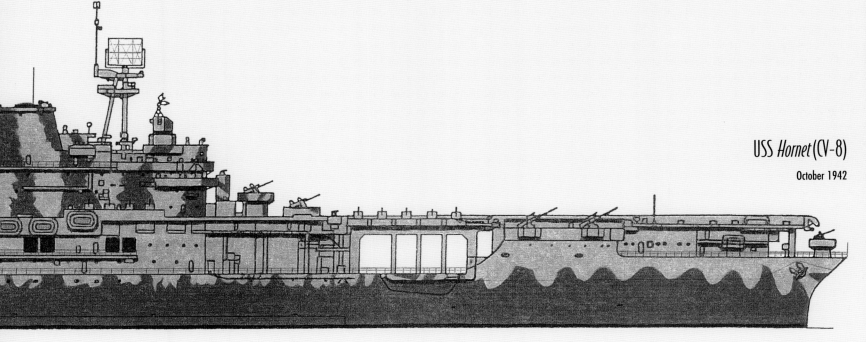

USS *Hornet* (CV-8)

October 1942

one under the command of Admiral Raymond A. Spruance (cruisers of this task force were separately commanded by Rear Admiral Thomas C. Kinkaid) and the other under the command of Rear Admiral Fletcher. In addition, there was a Marine Corps air group based on Midway, augmented by Army bombers from Hawaii.

The Japanese naval forces steaming toward Midway at the end of May 1942 consisted of five carriers, seven battleships, fourteen cruisers, forty-two destroyers, sixteen submarines, twelve troop transports (carrying 5,000 soldiers), and numerous support ships. The ships and submarines were divided into four different groups. The strongest of these four groups consisted of four large aircraft carriers with 261 planes, two battleships, three cruisers, twelve destroyers, and numerous support ships. The Japanese submarines were deployed in a large arc east and northeast of Midway to stop the U.S. Navy from interfering with the group of Japanese ships carrying the troop transports.

In an unsuccessful effort to divert U.S. Navy attention away from their Midway invasion operation, the Japanese Navy sent a fifth group of ships (including two aircraft carriers) to the American Aleutian Island chain. Japanese troops landed on the islands of Kiska and Attu, the closest they would ever come to the United States. Both islands would be reoccupied by American troops in 1943.

On the morning of June 3, Japanese naval forces on an easterly course were sighted several hundred miles southwest of Midway. The exact composition of the force was not known, but it was clearly a large attack force with supporting vessels. Late that afternoon, a formation of American B-17 four-engine bombers attacked the Japanese naval force with little success.

The next morning, American radar detected 108 Japanese aircraft heading toward the island of Midway from the northwest. At the same time, two of the four large Japanese carriers and the main body of the enemy were sighted in the same vicinity. While Japanese carrier aircraft successfully bombed Midway, they suffered heavy losses from American land-based fighter planes and anti-aircraft guns. Meanwhile, U.S. Army, Navy, and Marine Corps planes from Midway attacked the

Seen through a periscope of a U.S. Navy submarine, a torpedoed Japanese destroyer slowly sinks under the waves in June 1942. During the war, U.S. submarine attacks were not limited to Japanese warships; they also resulted in the destruction of more than 1,110 Japanese merchant ships. The loss of so many supply ships prevented Japanese industry from acquiring the raw materials—primarily oil, rubber, and minerals—that it needed to keep its economy running.

# Cruisers

During World War II, cruisers were generally viewed as utility ships that could operate alone, in groups, or with the fleet. When operating with the fleet, they provided concentrated anti-aircraft protection for other ships.

In the U.S. and Japanese navies, cruisers were divided into heavy and light ships solely on the basis of their armament and not their displacement. In the U.S. Navy, those cruisers mounting main guns larger than six inches (15cm)—a reference to the diameter of a gun's bore—were classified as heavy cruisers. Those with main guns smaller than six inches were classified as light cruisers.

RIGHT: One of the most decorated U.S. Navy cruisers to see service during World War II was the heavy cruiser *San Francisco*. It belonged to the seven ships of the New Orleans Class, all of which entered service between 1934 and 1936. The *San Francisco*, befitting its name, was built in the San Francisco Bay area, at the Mare Island Shipyard in Vallejo, California. The main armament of the ships in its class consisted of nine 8-inch (20cm) guns in three triple-armored turrets. This diagram depicts the changes in configuration to the ship's camouflage and radar equipment, from peacetime to war. The *San Francisco* survived the war only to be scrapped in 1959. OPPOSITE: A formation of U.S. Navy light cruisers of the Omaha Class steam along at high speed during a pre-World War II training exercise. The riveted armored turret in the foreground contains two 6-inch (15cm) guns. There were ten light cruisers of the Omaha Class built during World War I.

## USS *San Francisco* (CA-38)

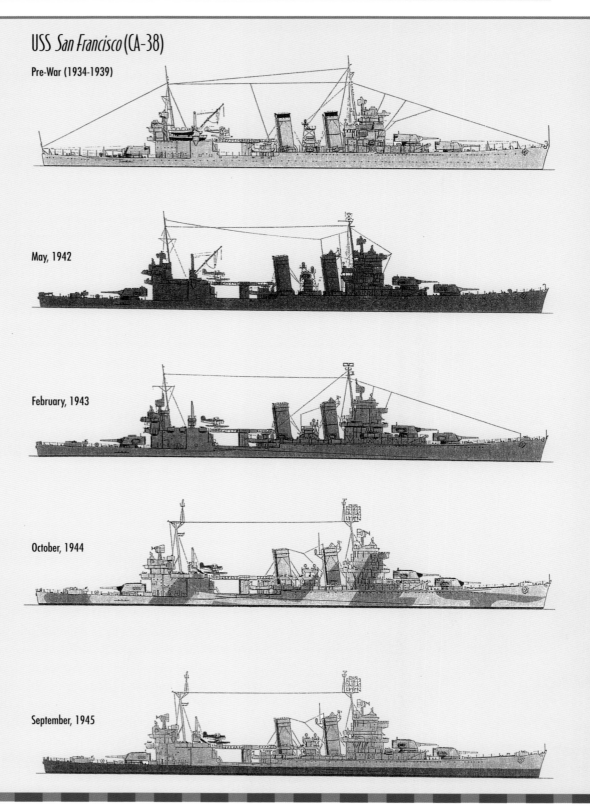

Pre-War (1934-1939)

May, 1942

February, 1943

October, 1944

September, 1945

RIGHT: U.S. Navy sailors on the island of Midway examine a Grumman TBF Avenger torpedo bomber damaged during the fighting around the island in June 1942. The Avenger had a three-man flight crew and could carry a single torpedo or 2,000 pounds (906kg) of conventional bombs.
OPPOSITE, TOP: Two U.S. Navy Douglas SBD Dauntless dive-bombers in flight during the Battle of Midway in June 1942. In the distance, a Japanese Navy aircraft carrier burns after being attacked by American planes. The Japanese Navy lost four carriers and hundreds of its best pilots, which it could not replace, during the Battle of Midway.
OPPOSITE, BOTTOM: Crewmen of the U.S. Navy aircraft carrier *Yorktown* abandon ship during the Battle of Midway in June 1942. A U.S. Navy destroyer stands by to rescue the survivors. During the battle, the *Yorktown* suffered two attacks by Japanese carrier aircraft that left it dead in the water. U.S. Navy efforts to tow the ship away from the area for repairs were cut short on June 6 when a Japanese submarine sneaked past a guard of destroyers and put two torpedoes into the ship. The *Yorktown* sank the following morning.

Japanese carriers, battleships, and other vessels, inflicting serious damage on at least one carrier.

At this point, the three U.S. Navy carriers joined the engagement. Torpedo Squadron 8 from the carrier *Hornet*, without the protection of fighters or dive-bombers, made the first attack on the four Japanese carriers. All planes in the squadron were shot down without scoring any hits on their intended targets. Only one man from the unit survived. About an hour later, torpedo squadrons from the carriers *Enterprise* and *Yorktown* registered hits on two Japanese carriers. They also suffered heavy losses. These attacks were followed by dive-bomber attacks from the *Enterprise* that took two Japanese carriers out of action. Bombers from the *Yorktown* severely damaged a third carrier, a cruiser, and a battleship. The damaged carrier was later sunk by a U.S. Navy submarine.

Planes from the remaining Japanese carrier then attacked the *Yorktown*, and although this attack force was annihilated, it succeeded in making three bomb hits. Shortly afterward, Japanese torpedo planes scored two fatal hits on the *Yorktown* and orders were given to abandon ship. About two hours later, planes from the *Enterprise* attacked the Japanese carrier and set her on fire. A second torpedo squadron from the *Hornet* found that the Japanese carrier was already damaged so badly that it no longer required their attention; instead, they could concentrate on a nearby Japanese battleship and a cruiser, both of which were hit.

At this stage of the engagement, it was apparent that the U.S. Navy, with help from the other services, had won control of the air, and it remained for the aircraft from Midway to perform cleanup operations. Army B-17 four-engine bombers set a Japanese heavy cruiser on fire.

Other planes scored hits on a battleship, the damaged carrier, and a destroyer. By the end of the day, the Japanese were fully defeated.

On the morning of June 5, aircraft from the *Enterprise* and the *Hornet* made an ineffective attack on a Japanese light cruiser. Planes from Midway scored a number of hits on two Japanese cruisers, one of which they crippled. Poor visibility that day prevented further operations.

On June 6, planes from the *Hornet* and the *Enterprise*, locating a Japanese force consisting of two cruisers and three destroyers, made hits on the cruisers. Later in the day, planes from the *Hornet* successfully attacked two more cruisers and a destroyer. On the same day, in an effort to save the *Yorktown*, the destroyer *Hammann* went alongside to put a salvage party on board. While the destroyer was in that position, two torpedoes from a Japanese submarine struck the carrier. The *Hammann* was also hit by a torpedo, and it sank within minutes. The *Yorktown* sank the next morning.

The Battle of Midway was the first decisive defeat suffered by the Japanese Navy in 350 years. It also put an end to a long period of Japanese offensive action and restored the balance of naval power in the Pacific. The threat to Hawaii was removed, and except for minor operations in the Aleutians, Japanese operations were confined to the South Pacific, where the U.S. Navy soon focused its attention.

# Chapter 4

# The Central Pacific Advance

AT THE END OF AUGUST 1943, ADMIRAL CHESTER A. NIMITZ BEGAN ORGANIZING the Pacific Fleet for its first large-scale amphibious assault on a Japanese outpost in the Central Pacific. This endeavor would mark the first time that American military forces in the Pacific would mount concurrent operations in both the Southwest Pacific and the Central Pacific areas.

The target selected was the Gilbert Islands—part of the Japanese outer defensive perimeter in the Central Pacific composed of sixteen atolls located roughly 2,000 miles (3,218km) southwest of Pearl Harbor. This chain of islands had been under British control since 1892, but this changed three days after the Pearl Harbor attack, when a small force of Japanese military personnel assumed occupation. These forces soon established a seaplane base on Makin Atoll and also placed a token force at Tarawa Atoll. (The word "atoll" is used to mean both a singular coral island and a larger group of such land masses.) They also installed coast watchers on some of the other atolls. From this location, the Japanese could endanger the long seaborne supply line between the United States and Australia.

A raid on Makin Atoll by U.S. Marine Corps commandos in August 1942 had convinced the Japanese that the United States had attached a great deal more importance to the Gilbert Islands

LEFT: U.S. Army soldiers wade toward the shore of the burning island of Butaritari, part of the Makin Atoll, on November 20, 1943. At the same time that U.S. Army troops were attempting to secure Butaritari, a much larger force of U.S. Marines was attempting to seize the island of Betio, part of the Tarawa Atoll, 105 miles (168km) south of the Makin Atoll.

OPPOSITE: U.S. Marines take cover from Japanese fire on one of the invasion beaches on the island of Betio, part of the Gilbert Islands' Tarawa Atoll. Betio was the most heavily defended Japanese position in the Gilbert Islands. It took the Marine Corps three days to secure, at a cost of more than 3,000 casualties. LEFT: U.S. Marines make the final attack on a large, bombproof Japanese shelter on the island of Betio. Earlier assaults on the Japanese position were beaten back with heavy losses to the Marines. Finally, a squad of Marine combat engineers reached the top of the shelter and dropped explosives and grenades down the air vents, forcing the Japanese defenders to flee their position into the open. Once out of the shelter, the occupying troops were cut to pieces by Marine Corps fire.

than the Japanese had initially assumed. In response, the Japanese quickly sent in a large force of their elite Special Naval Landing Forces (the Japanese equivalent of the Marine Corps). The bulk of these men and their equipment was stationed on Betio, the principal island in the Tawara Atoll. Secondary attention was also devoted to defending Makin and Apamama atolls.

The commander of the Japanese Imperial Marines on Betio, Rear Admiral Tomanari Saichiro, a top-notch engineer, directed the construction of 500 integrated pillboxes, blockhouses, and other emplacements on Betio. These defensive positions were armed with whatever the Japanese could spare—from machine guns to British-made 8-inch (20cm) coastal artillery guns, acquired by Japan in 1905. The Japanese also placed a small number of tanks on Betio. Admiral Saichiro proudly boasted to his troops, "A million Americans couldn't take Tarawa in 100 years." His

optimism was understandable, since Betio was the most heavily defended atoll in the Pacific.

To carry out the 1943 assault on the Gilbert Islands, Nimitz appointed Vice Admiral Raymond A. Spruance as commander of the newly formed Fifth Fleet. Rear Admiral Richmond K. Turner commanded the U.S. Navy amphibious forces and Marine Corps Major General Julian C. Smith commanded the landing forces. In total, these leaders would have at their disposal more than 200 vessels, including ten aircraft carriers, five brand-new battleships, six cruisers, and twenty-one destroyers. The amphibious landings would be carried out by the Second Marine Division with help from the U.S. Army Twenty-seventh Infantry Division.

On November 19, 1943, U.S. Navy cruisers bombarded Tarawa Atoll, and on the morning of November 20, Navy attack groups were located a short distance off the coasts of both Tarawa and Makin atolls. Heavy shore

A terrible sight: Marines look out over a part of the island of Betio littered with the bodies of dead comrades. The average casualty rate among the Marines engaged in the assault on the island was about 19 percent, a steep but "acceptable" price, according to those who planned the invasion. Some Marine units, however, suffered more than 50 percent losses. The Marine Corps carefully reviewed the costly mistakes made on Betio and were better prepared for future amphibious operations.

bombardments by U.S. Navy battleships and cruisers preceded the landing at Makin, located 105 miles (169km) north of Tarawa. U.S. Army troops who landed on the island met little opposition at first, but the Japanese eventually put up a stiff fight. The success of this maneuver, however, was never in serious doubt. The capture of Makin was announced on November 22.

The November 20 assault on Betio in the Tarawa Atoll was a different story. This maneuver was not expected to be easy, but it turned out to be far more difficult than predicted. Despite an intense naval shore and

air bombardment that lasted two and a half hours, the Japanese defenders and most of their fortified positions survived intact. Of the 5,000 U.S. Marines who fought in the first assault wave, 1,500 were dead, wounded, or missing by the end of the first day.

The situation on Betio remained precarious for much of the second day of the assault. The defenders fiercely repelled all Marine efforts to land reinforcements or to enlarge their small beachhead. The stench of dead bodies covered the island and even drifted out to sea, where additional Marines prepared for landing.

On the third day, with a larger Marine force on the island, the tide of battle finally began to turn. This was reflected in the last Japanese radio message from Betio:

> *Our weapons have been destroyed and from now on everybody is attempting a final charge. May Japan exist for 10,000 years.*

That night, the Japanese mounted a series of desperate counterattacks against Marine positions. They took such heavy losses in these attacks that by the morning of November 23 their remaining forces were confined to a small area at the eastern tip of the island and were quickly eliminated.

In the end, the final American casualty figures for the capture of Betio included 1,009 killed and 2,101 wounded. Of the 4,856 men that made up the Japanese garrison, 4,690 lay dead. Most of the 146 prisoners taken on the island were conscripted Korean laborers. Only seventeen Japanese Marines surrendered.

## The Marshall Islands

The next target for Admiral Nimitz in the Central Pacific was the Marshall Islands, roughly 600 miles (965km) northwest of the Gilberts. American control of the Marshalls would significantly weaken the Japanese outer defensive perimeter.

The Marshall Islands consist of thirty-two atolls, more than 1,000 islands, and 867 reefs. The largest of the Marshall atolls is Kwajalein: 60 miles (97km) long and 20 miles (32km) wide, it is the world's largest atoll. Kwajalein and the two connected islands of Roi and Namur were chosen for Marine amphibious landings.

On December 4, 1943, in preparation for the Kwajalein invasion, the U.S. Navy began a series of carrier raids directed against the Japanese-occupied Marshall Islands. During the remainder of the year, U.S. Army and Navy land-based planes from the Gilbert Islands carried out repeated attacks on Japanese positions in the Marshall Islands, inflicting considerable damage on ships and shore installations. The Japanese retaliated with air attacks on American bases in the Gilbert Islands, but no serious damage was sustained.

ABOVE: On the flight deck of the U.S. Navy aircraft carrier *Saratoga* in November 1943, a plane handler guides a Grumman F6F Hellcat fighter into position on an elevator that will take it down to the ship's hangar deck. LEFT: A struggling Japanese soldier who refused to surrender is carried back to a rear area headquarters unit for questioning by a U.S. soldier. Because the Japanese were taught that surrendering to an enemy would bring everlasting shame upon themselves and their families, soldiers fought to the death on most occasions.

# Amphibious Tractors

One of the unique vehicles that made possible the amphibious landings in the Central Pacific and Southwest Pacific campaigns was the amphibious tractor. In official naval terms, it was referred to as the Landing Vehicle Tracked (LVT). Nicknames were attached to the LVT in service, including alligator, water buffalo, amtrak, amtrac, or amphtrac.

During World War II, several different manufacturers produced LVTs in a variety of progressively improved versions (LVT-1 through LVT-5). By war's end the total production of all types amounted to 18,620 vehicles. LVTs would come in both armored and unarmored versions. Armaments on LVTs varied from exposed machine guns to turret-mounted 75-mm howitzers. In the Pacific, both the Marine Corps and U.S. Army used LVTs.

An LVT(A)2 amphibious tractor loaded with Marines churns through choppy sea to make an assault on the island of Tinian in July 1944. The letter designation "A" stood for "armored."

On February 1, 1944, following a massive pre-landing saturation bombardment by U.S. Navy aircraft and warships that lasted more than two days, Marines landed on the islands of Roi and Namur. Marine Lieutenant John C. Chapin recalled some of the events of the first assault wave:

> By now everything was all mixed up, with our assault wave all entangled with the armored tractors [LVTs] ahead of us. I ordered my driver to maneuver around them. Slowly we inched past, as their 37-mm guns and .50-caliber machine guns flamed. The beach lay right before us. However, it was shrouded in such a pall of dust and smoke from our bombardment that we could see very little of it. As a result, we were unable to tell which section we were approaching (after all our hours of careful planning, based on hitting the beach at one exact spot!). I turned to talk to my platoon sergeant, who was manning the machine gun right behind me. He was slumped over—the whole right side of his face disintegrated into a mass of gore. Up to now, the entire operation had seemed almost like a movie, or like one of the innumerable practice landings we'd made.

Despite the misfortune that fell upon Chapin and his men during this assault, the invasion was met with minor Japanese resistance, compared with the fighting that had consumed Tarawa ten weeks before. Roi fell on the first day; Namur was taken on the second day.

Simultaneous with the Marine landing on Roi and Namur, soldiers from the U.S. Army Seventh Infantry Division stormed ashore on Kwajalein. In the face of fanatic Japanese resistance, the American soldiers fought for four days to clear the atoll of Japanese troops. Of the roughly 4,000 Japanese defenders on Kwajalein, only 100 survived long enough to surrender, along with 165 Korean laborers.

By February 7, the numerous islands that surround Kwajalein were all in American hands. Army and Marine casualties were surprisingly light when compared to those suffered during the operations in the Gilbert Islands. Of the 41,000 troops committed to the operation, 372 were killed and 1,582 wounded.

With 10,000 uncommitted reserve troops still on board their troop transport ships, Admiral Nimitz decided to conduct an early amphibious invasion of Eniwetok Atoll (part of the Marshall Island chain, located 330 miles [531km] northeast of Kwajalein).

The original invasion schedule had called for a large amphibious landing by U.S. naval forces on Eniwetok Atoll and its surrounding islands during the month of May. With fresh troops already in the area, the Eniwetok invasion was rescheduled for immediate implementation.

A heavy pre-invasion aerial bombardment of Eniwetok Atoll had been in progress since the end of January 1944. A Japanese soldier, forced to endure the constant bombing, wrote in his diary:

*The American attacks are becoming more furious. Planes come over day after day. Can we stand up under the strain?*

Another noted that:

*Some soldiers have gone out of their minds.*

American assault troops began their invasion of Eniwetok Atoll and its surrounding islands in a carefully planned sequence of attacks beginning on February 17, 1944. By February 21 the area was secured.

A group of Marines hug the ground as they wait for the blast from an M1A1 portable flamethrower to do its dirty work before assaulting a Japanese defensive position in the Central Pacific. The effectiveness of the portable flamethrowers was limited by the weapon's range of only 45 to 50 yards (41–46m). The need to approach a target so closely resulted in high casualty rates for the operators.

Aboard an older model U.S. Navy battleship during World War II, the crews of a battery of Mark 7 5-inch (12cm) anti-aircraft guns prepare themselves for action. The Mark 7 fired a 50-pound (23kg) high-explosive shell up to an altitude of more than 20,000 feet (6,080m). Later models of the weapon were deployed in twin mounts and enclosed within power-operated armored turrets.

RIGHT: A rifle marks the spot where a U.S. Marine lies dead on a beach of Eniwetok Atoll. The Marine Corps assault on the atoll and its assorted islands, located in the Western Marshall Islands, began on February 19, 1944, and ended on February 23. Some 3,400 Japanese soldiers were killed, compared with 348 Americans killed and 866 wounded.
BELOW: Demonstrating the savage nature of the fighting in the Pacific, a dead Marine, killed by a sniper, clutches the bayonet he used to kill the Japanese soldier in the background.

## Marine Corps Tanks

The Marine Corps has always been very concerned about providing its men on the ground with as much firepower as possible. One of the best ways to accomplish that goal was with heavily armed tanks.

The first offensive deployment of Marine tanks took place on Guadalcanal in August 1942. At the time, the Marines were using the 15-ton (13,620kg) M-3 Stuart light tanks, each armed with a 37-mm gun and at least two machine guns. Lacking proper antitank weapons, Japanese infantrymen would climb onto the tanks and try to open the hatches so that they could fire into the tanks. They were usually picked off by machine gun fire from other tanks or by "friendly fire."

In 1943, the Marines began replacing their light tanks with 32-ton (29,056kg) M-4 Sherman medium tanks, whenever possible. The Sherman was armed with a 75-mm gun and at least two machine guns. Some of the Marine Corps Sherman tanks were also fitted with flame-throwers. Due to the small numbers of Japanese tanks in the Pacific, the primary role of Marine Corps tanks was infantry support.

A Marine Corps Stuart light tank supports Marine infantry in the Marshall Islands in early 1944.

# The Mariana Islands

After the capture of Eniwetok, the Joint Chiefs decided that the southern Mariana Islands, located 1,000 miles (1,609km) west of the Marshall Islands, would be the next Central Pacific objective. Control of the Marianas was a crucial element of the Japanese inner defensive perimeter. Of the many islands that make up the chain, the three largest islands, Saipan, Tinian, and Guam, were the ones targeted by the Joint Chiefs. Saipan was the first objective, since the loss of its airfield would allow Vice Admiral Spruance's Fifth Fleet carriers to establish air dominance over the entire region.

Admiral Nimitz saw the occupation of the Mariana Islands as a chance to "initiate the isolation and neutralization of the central Carolines." Within these islands lay the Japanese stronghold at Truk Atoll, home of the main Japanese Fleet since July 1942. The base at Truk also supported a large fleet of bombers.

At the same time Eniwetok was being assaulted, Nimitz launched a massive attack on Truk. Carrier-based planes attacked first on February 17. The next day, battleships, cruisers, and destroyers joined the attack. Heavy damage was inflicted on the Japanese. Merchant ships were sunk or severely damaged, and planes were shot down or destroyed on the ground.

The appearance of U.S. Navy reconnaissance planes over Truk in early February had alerted the Japanese that an American attack was pending. Most of the Japanese warships in the area quickly departed for other bases. During its attack on Truk, the U.S. Navy sank only four Japanese cruisers and two destroyers.

The invasion date for Saipan was set for June 15, 1944. Guam was to follow on June 18. The invasion schedule for Tinian would depend on the progress at Saipan and Guam, because some of the same troops would be involved. The Joint Chiefs envisioned a number of dividends from taking over the three main islands of the Marianas, including the following:

1. The interruption of the Japanese aerial pipeline to the Carolina Island chain, located south of the Mariana Islands.
2. The development of new surface and submarine bases for the U.S. Navy Pacific Fleet.

3. The establishment of a B-29 heavy bomber base from which to bomb the Japanese home islands.
4. The occupation of a position from which there would be a choice of several different objectives for the next operation, thereby keeping the Japanese uncertain of American intentions.
5. The penetration of the Japanese inner defense perimeter (about 1,200 miles [1,931km] from Tokyo), which might force a decisive engagement with the Japanese fleet.

For the assault on the Mariana Islands, Admiral Nimitz would employ the Fifth Fleet, which had now grown to more than 106 warships and hundreds of support ships. The troop transports of the Fifth Fleet were carrying three reinforced Marine divisions and one reinforced Army division—a grand total of more than 127,500 troops.

U.S. Marines crawl along a Saipan Island beach on June 24, 1944, while trying to dodge Japanese fire. A U.S. Navy landing craft hit by enemy artillery fire burns in the background. The large island of Saipan, part of the Mariana island chain, formed an important part of Japan's inner defensive perimeter around the home islands.

The Marine Corps crew of an M3A1 37-mm antitank gun prepares to fire at Japanese defensive positions on Saipan in June 1944. The M3A1, mounted on a two-wheel towed carriage, weighed 912 pounds (413kg) and fired a huge armor-piercing projectile up to 500 yards (456m). Though this weapon was obsolete in Europe—it did little damage against the heavily armored German tanks—it remained effective against Japanese tanks to the end of the Second World War.

On the morning of June 15, the first wave of Marines headed for the beaches of Saipan. The roughly 25,000 Japanese defenders waited patiently—positive that they could trounce the assault troops. As the Marines aboard their amphibious tractors and assorted landing craft reached the reef surrounding the island, all hell broke loose. The Japanese opened fire with artillery, mortars, and small arms. Despite the heavy Japanese barrage, more than 8,000 Marines managed to make it ashore in the first twenty minutes and set up beachhead positions. By that afternoon, the Marines had 20,000 men and supporting artillery on the island.

Despite their success in the Saipan landing on the first day of the invasion, the Marines knew that they still faced a grueling battle. On the night of the second day, a fleet of forty-four Japanese tanks launched a major attack against the Marines. Marine Corps Major James A. Donovan later described the wild clash:

*The battle evolved itself into a madhouse of noise, tracers, and flashing lights. As [Japanese] tanks were hit and set afire, they silhouetted other tanks coming out of the flickering shadows to the front or already on top of the squads.*

Using bazookas, grenade launchers, tanks, and artillery, the Marines repelled the Japanese armor attack. The next morning, the Americans found the shattered hulks of twenty-four enemy tanks on the battlefield in front of their defensive positions.

On July 9, Saipan was officially declared secured. American losses included 3,255 dead, 13,061 wounded, and 326 missing. Japanese losses were estimated at

24,000. Only 736 enemy prisoners were taken, and 438 of them were Korean laborers.

# The Battle of the Philippine Sea

Since the beginning of the war, the Japanese Navy had welcomed the opportunity for a decisive fleet engagement with the U.S. Navy in the Pacific—under the right conditions. One purpose of the ill-fated Japanese Midway venture had been to bring about a fleet action while the U.S. Navy was still weak. By 1944, the Japanese Navy was clearly the weaker of the two navies. Still, senior leaders of the Japanese Navy thought a great naval victory was still possible, and they wanted to prove it.

When the U.S. Navy launched a series of carrier air strikes on the Mariana Islands on June 11, the Japanese admirals saw their chance. Unfortunately for them, an American submarine crew spotted the Japanese naval buildup and alerted Admiral Spruance's Fifth Fleet that something big was happening.

On the afternoon of June 16, Spruance informed his senior commanders that "The Japanese are coming after us." He also called off the June 18 landing on Guam. By the evening of June 17, American radio direction finders placed the Japanese fleet 600 miles (965km) west of Guam.

On June 19, the carrier air arms of the two opposing fleets met. Surprisingly, American pilots did not spot the Japanese fleet prior to the day of the battle. The submarine fleet again saved the day. The submarines *Albacore* and *Cavalla* located the Japanese fleet and sank two of its nine carriers with torpedoes.

The actions on that day consisted of a series of large air battles that left the Japanese in shock. Of the 430 Japanese planes (including some ground-based aircraft) launched against the American Fifth Fleet, 330 were lost in battle. American losses amounted to only 17 planes, and only four ships suffered minor damage. Exultant U.S. Navy pilots called the conflict "The Great Marianas Turkey Shoot."

Late in the afternoon of the next day, a force of 216 American carrier planes pursued the fast-retreating Japanese fleet, and in a matter of minutes they sank one additional Japanese carrier and three tankers, badly damaged two other carriers, and heavily damaged two cruisers. Of the eighty Japanese carrier planes launched in response to the American attack, sixty-five were shot down.

Since the U.S. carrier pilots who took part in the attack on the retreating Japanese fleet had taken off from the extreme limits of their theoretical attack range, many of the surviving planes ran out of fuel and crashed into the sea before they could make it back to the carriers. Of the 216 planes that went out, eighty planes were shot down, crashed on landing (it was dark and the carriers unlit for fear of enemy submarines), or plunged into the sea when they ran out of fuel (though in the latter case almost all the crews were saved). Eventually, the carrier commanders made the decision to illuminate the landing decks to help the remainder of the returning planes land safely.

On the first evening of the Marine Corps invasion of the island of Saipan, the Japanese mounted a major counterattack with forty-four tanks. In the desperate nightlong struggle that followed, the Marines managed to turn back the Japanese tanks with a combination of fire from their own tanks, bazookas, and self-propelled 75-mm antitank guns mounted on half-tracks. Pictured is a destroyed Type Chi-Ha medium tank armed with a turret-mounted 57-mm gun.

*As the night wore on, the intensity of enemy attacks started to build and build and build. They finally launched a full-scale banzai attack against [our] battalion. The strange thing the Japanese did here was that they executed one wave of attack after another against a 37-mm position firing cannister ammunition.*

*That gun just stacked up dead Japanese. As soon as one Marine gunner would drop, another would take his place. [Eight of ten men who manned the gun were killed or wounded.] Soon, we were nearly shoulder-high with dead Japanese in front of that weapon. By morning we had defeated the enemy. Around us were lots of dead ones, hundreds of them as a matter of fact. From then on, we were able to finish the rest of the campaign without difficulty. People have said that the Tinian campaign was the easiest campaign in the Pacific.*

On August 1 the island was declared secure. Japanese losses were estimated at 5,000 or more. Counting was difficult because so many had been sealed up inside caves and underground fortifications. American losses included 105 killed and 655 wounded.

ABOVE: Marines scramble for cover from Japanese fire during the invasion of Guam on July 24, 1944. Like Saipan, Guam is part of the Mariana island chain in the Central Pacific. Due to strong enemy resistance and the varied geography of the island, with its many places to hide, organized Japanese resistance was not eliminated until August 10. OPPOSITE: U.S. Marines on Guam prepare to move off one of the invasion beaches while under Japanese fire. Guam was 35 miles (56km) long, 9 miles (14.4km) at its widest point, and 4 miles (6.4km) at its narrowest. After the invasion of Saipan—and a month-long bombardment by U.S. ships and planes— the Japanese knew Guam was next.

# Finishing off the Mariana Islands

With the threat from the Japanese fleet now gone, the invasion of Guam proceeded on July 21, 1944. Although Japanese opposition was stubborn, it did not reach the intensity encountered on Saipan, and by August 10 all organized resistance on the island ceased. Japanese losses were put at 11,000 men. Another 9,000 remained alive in small scattered bands hidden in the jungles and hills. It took months for American soldiers to root out these stragglers, and some isolated groups were not found until after the war ended. American casualties on Guam included 1,744 killed or missing and another 5,930 wounded.

Tinian, located across a narrow channel to the southwest of Saipan, was invaded by two Marine Corps divisions on July 24. They met with only light rifle and mortar fire, and quickly set up a strong beachhead position. As on Saipan and Guam, the rough terrain on Tinian presented some problems, but Japanese resistance was much less stubborn and more disorganized than on the other islands.

Marine Captain Carl W. Hoffman described the fighting on Tinian as follows:

# The Western Caroline Islands

With the Mariana Islands safely in American hands, Admiral Nimitz set his sights on the islands of Palau, the westernmost of the Caroline Island chain, located some 500 miles (805km) east of the Philippines. Within the Palau Islands, the island of Peleliu became the primary objective because of a very large Japanese airfield. A secondary target was the nearby island of Angaur, seen as an excellent location to build an airfield for bombers. Nimitz believed that the capture of these islands was necessary to protect MacArthur's southern flank during his planned invasion of Leyte Island in the Philippines.

The landing on the island of Peleliu took place on September 15, 1944, following a strong preparatory bombardment. In spite of difficult reef conditions, the Marines quickly overran the Japanese beach defenses,

which were thickly mined but less heavily manned than expected. By the second night of the invasion, the Japanese-built airfield on the island had been taken by U.S. forces.

After the rapid conquest of the southern portion of the island, American progress on Peleliu slowed to a crawl in the face of increasingly tougher Japanese resistance. Part of the problem was the towering lime-stone ridges that formed the north-south backbone of the island. The Japanese had turned these ridges into a natural fortress consisting of numerous cave positions organized in successive defensive lines of soldiers armed with a wide variety of automatic weapons. Marines who attempted to advance along the tall ridgeline did not survive.

By the end of September, the northern portion of Peleliu was declared secure, although it took another two months for U.S. Army cleanup crews to quash the last organized Japanese resistance on the island. Of the roughly 11,000 enemy personnel on Peleliu before the American invasion, only 406 survived, and most of these were Korean laborers. American casualties included 1,685 killed and 6,965 wounded.

The assault on the island of Angaur by soldiers of the U.S. Army's Eighty-first Infantry Division began on September 17, 1944, and resulted in no surprises. By noon on September 20, the Japanese occupiers—except for a few holdouts in a rough patch of terrain—had been defeated.

# Chapter 5

# Back to the Philippines

HAVING SECURED THE ADMIRALTIES IN MARCH 1944, MACARTHUR BYPASSED strong Japanese positions at Wewak and Hansa Bay and landed his forces at Hollandia, New Guinea, in April 1944, two months ahead of his original schedule.

The amphibious assault on Hollandia began at first light on April 22. By June 6, the last Japanese resistance was overcome. American casualties amounted to only 124 men killed, 1,057 wounded, and twenty-eight missing in action. Japanese casualties were estimated at 3,300 killed, 611 captured, and an unknown number of wounded.

The seizure of Hollandia and the surrounding areas brought MacArthur's strategic plan for the approach to the Philippines one step closer to realization. The Americans set up an airfield along the New Guinea coast to provide air cover for forces farther afield. By May 1944 MacArthur's forces, taking advantage of this, had jumped ahead another 125 miles (201km) to Wakda Island, located off the New Guinea coast.

Wakda had a Japanese-built airfield whose capture would prove most useful to MacArthur's operations in New Guinea. The island itself was only 3,000 yards (2,743m) long and 1,200 yards (1,097m) wide, and had been a coconut plantation before

LEFT: On the afternoon of October 20, 1944, after the first few waves of U.S. troops had pushed inland on the Philippine island of Leyte, General Douglas MacArthur decided to leave the U.S. Navy cruiser *Nashville* and travel ashore by landing craft. Accompanying MacArthur were a number of Philippine officials, media representatives, and members of his staff. In this famous picture, MacArthur finally returns to Philippine soil.

The U.S. advance along the New Guinea coastline on the way to the Philippines has been all but forgotten except by those who served there. Better-known Pacific Ocean battles with names like Tarawa and Iwo Jima have been covered in more detail. For those who did serve under MacArthur's command in New Guinea, it is the terrain and the climate that are best remembered. There were no roads or railroads on the island of New Guinea. Supply lines consisted only of dirt trails that could disappear in a few minutes of torrential tropical rain. And soldiers were pushed to their physical limits, forced to stagger along carrying 60 pounds (27kg) of gear in temperatures reaching the mid-90s (around 35°C) with humidity levels to match.

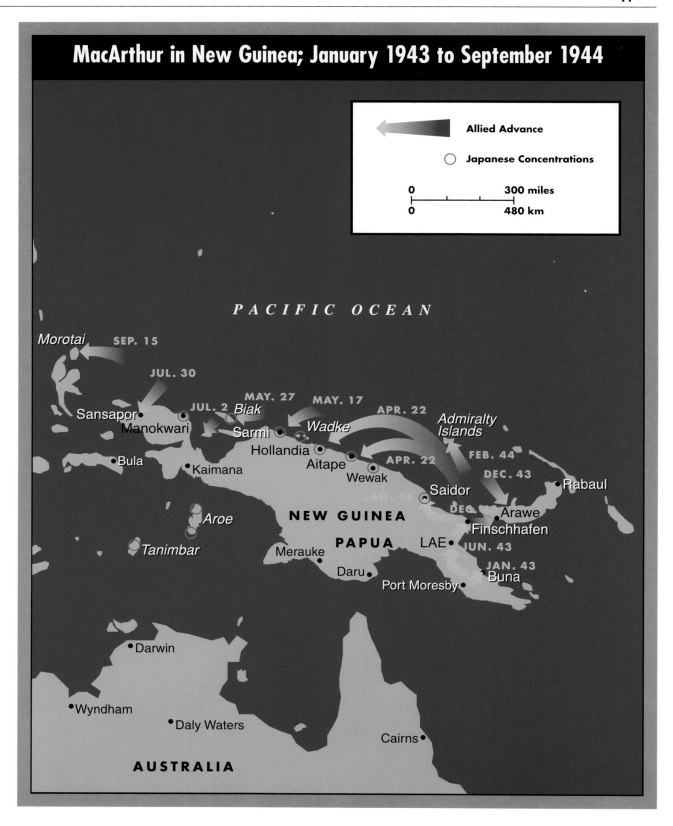

# MacArthur in New Guinea; January 1943 to September 1944

Allied Advance

○ Japanese Concentrations

| 0 | 300 miles |
| 0 | 480 km |

PACIFIC OCEAN

Morotai   SEP. 15

JUL. 30

MAY. 27   MAY. 17

JUL. 2   *Biak*   APR. 22   *Admiralty Islands*

Sansapor   *Wadke*

Manokwari   Sarmi

  Hollandia   APR. 22   FEB. 44

Bula   Aitape   DEC. 43

Kaimana   Wewak   Rabaul

JAN. 44   Saidor

*Aroe*   NEW GUINEA   DEC.   Arawe

  Finschhafen

PAPUA   LAE   JUN. 43

*Tanimbar*   Merauke   JAN. 43

Daru   Buna

Port Moresby

Darwin

Wyndham

Daly Waters

Cairns

**AUSTRALIA**

the war. The island was invaded by MacArthur's forces on May 18, 1944, and was declared secure the next day. The airfield was made operational on May 21.

Ten days after the capture of Wakda, MacArthur's amphibious forces landed on Biak Island (325 miles [523km] northwest of Hollandia) with the goal of capturing the five Japanese-built airfields on the island. More than 11,000 Japanese personnel occupied Biak Island, but only 4,000 of them were combat troops. Unlike the relatively easy conquests of Hollandia and Wakda Island, the Japanese defenders of Biak surprised

MacArthur's commanders with a tough fight. So fierce were the Japanese counterattacks on the island of Biak that some American units were forced to retreat from their positions.

It took until June 8, 1944, for the heavily reinforced American troops on Biak Island to capture the first enemy airfield. However, the Americans failed to seize the area surrounding the airfield, so American aircraft could not use it safely. By the middle of the month, the failure to have an operational airfield on Biak was starting to worry MacArthur and his commanders. Further

A U.S. Army 37-mm antitank gun on the large island of New Guinea fires at nearby Japanese positions. New Guinea was a horrible place to campaign. On the northern side of the island, the center for most of the ground fighting between 1942 and 1944, rainfall runs as high as 300 inches (7.6m) per year.

U.S. Navy PT-Boats armed with torpedoes and an assortment of small-caliber weapons played a major part in the fighting during the Solomon Island campaign and the conquest of New Guinea. Made out of wood and powered by three twelve-cylinder Packard marine engines, the PT-Boats could reach speeds of up to 40 knots. ✴

delays in the ability to use the captured airfields on Biak would threaten the timetable of future American operations in the Southwest Pacific.

Before the invasion of Biak, MacArthur's staff had considered occupying other islands in the surrounding area to protect their hard-fought gains and to provide an additional air base for an attack on the Vogelkop Peninsula, the last Japanese stronghold on northern New Guinea. On June 4, 1944, MacArthur's staff chose

the island of Noemfoor to expand operations in the area. Noemfoor is located on the northeast tip of the Vogelkop Peninsula, about halfway between the island of Biak and Manokwari, the site of two Japanese-built airstrips needed by MacArthur.

The attack on Noemfoor began on July 2. Unorganized Japanese resistance didn't last long, and the island was declared secure on August 31. Japanese casualties were estimated at 1,730 killed, and another 186 soldiers

*Jack Kennedy was C.O. on PT 109 which was splintered in the dark by a Japanese ship. It didn't sink. Survivors hung on to parts of it for hours. J.F.K. saved a burned sailor carrying him on his back, swimming, when it finally did sink. JZ*

were captured. American casualties included 63 killed, 343 wounded, and three missing in action.

The main Japanese airfield on Noemfoor was unsuitable for heavy use, so work was immediately begun on a new airfield. This job was completed by September 2. American aircraft flying from the new airfield would support MacArthur's invasions of the Vogelkop Peninsula and Morotai Island.

MacArthur saw the capture of the Vogelkop Peninsula as the final large-scale operation necessary for New Guinea. With the building of new airfields on the Vogelkop, American planes were able to support future operations in the Mindanao area of the Philippines. MacArthur's forces landed on the Vogelkop on July 30, 1944, and encountered little Japanese opposition. By August 31 the ground operations were concluded, except for some minor patrolling.

In mid-September, MacArthur deployed his forces to capture the lightly defended island of Morotai, located between New Guinea and the Philippine island of Mindanao. After Morotai was captured, MacArthur built a large naval supply base and a number of airfields on

ABOVE: American soldiers in New Guinea stand guard along a jungle stream with an air-cooled Browning M1919A4 .30-caliber machine gun. MacArthur's campaign to seize the northeast coast of New Guinea was completed by September 1944. In a period of nine months, MacArthur's forces had advanced more than 1,300 miles (2,080km). Allied casualties were just over 20,000, while Japanese losses were estimated at 43,000.
LEFT: A formation of U.S. Army Air Forces Douglas twin-engine A-20 Havoc attack bombers heads back to base following a successful bomb run on a Japanese-occupied village along the New Guinea coast.

the island, from which his ground-based aircraft could protect and support his invasion forces during their assault on Mindanao.

The main island of Luzon was still the key strategic objective in the Philippines. MacArthur and the Joint Chiefs had planned to make their first Philippine foot-hold on southern Mindanao, as far as possible from Japanese air and naval bases on Luzon. After Mindanao was secure, MacArthur planned to take the island of Leyte in mid-December. From Leyte, MacArthur would be able to establish further bases from which to eventually gain air supremacy over Luzon.

In September, however, MacArthur changed this plan when Admiral Halsey, with his fast carriers in support of the landings on the Palau Islands and Morotai, reported few signs of enemy ground, naval, or air activity.

MacArthur and Admiral Nimitz agreed that the immediate capture of Leyte was feasible. The Joint Chiefs, then meeting with the British Chiefs of Staff in Quebec, Canada, quickly issued the necessary orders. The attack on Mindanao and a second assault planned against Yap Island were both canceled. The Third Amphibious Forces, a U.S. Army corps of three divisions scheduled for the Yap invasion, were added to MacArthur's forces for the assault on Leyte. The decision to go to Leyte was strategically desirable, since it would force the Japanese to split their forces in the Philippines and virtually compel the Japanese Fleet to come out into the open to meet this threat to their inner defensive line.

MacArthur's forces went ashore at Leyte Gulf on October 20, 1944, in the largest amphibious assault ever conducted in the Pacific. To prevent Leyte from falling into enemy hands, the Japanese did exactly what the

Americans had anticipated—they diverted their remaining air and naval forces from Luzon to Leyte. The Japanese once again planned to destroy the American naval presence in the Pacific in one great battle. To maintain their local air superiority and to interrupt American shipping in the Leyte Gulf, the Japanese also reinforced their land-based air forces in the Philippines.

There soon followed a series of fierce naval engagements, collectively referred to as the Battle for Leyte Gulf. This so-called battle, which took place between October 23 and 26, actually consisted of four separate naval actions, including the Battle in the Sibuyan Sea, the Battle of Surigao Strait, the Battle of Samar, and the Battle of Cape Engano. These four sea battles amounted to the largest joint series of naval-military encounters in naval history.

The Battle for Leyte Gulf destroyed what remained of the Japanese Navy, which lost four aircraft carriers, three battleships, 10 cruisers, several destroyers and submarines, and almost 350 aircraft. U.S. Navy losses consisted of three carriers, two destroyers, a destroyer escort, and a submarine.

## Amphibious Operations

The function of the U.S. Navy in amphibious operations during World War II fell into four main phases.

- In the "approach" phase, the Navy commanded passage to the area of landing for the invasion forces; bombarded enemy shore batteries, landing beaches, and supporting areas; conducted minesweeping operations; and removed beach obstacles.
- In the "landing" phase, the Navy put the invasion forces ashore, under cover of ships' guns and carrier aircraft.
- In the "support" phase, the Navy continued to provide artillery and air support to the forces ashore for as long a time as those land forces remained within range of ships' guns, and until shore-based fighter squadrons could step in and relieve the carriers of the task of air support.
- In the "supply" phase, the Navy guaranteed the security of the supply lines of the invasion force and stopped any enemy efforts to reinforce their troops by sea.

The various types of U.S. Navy vessels used to bring troops and equipment onto enemy beaches were generally slow, unarmored, and had little armament with which to defend themselves. To provide the close offensive firepower needed to suppress Japanese coastal defense weapons, the Navy often employed destroyers like the *Lardner*, a Fletcher Class destroyer.

There was another type ship, the destroyer escort, a smaller ship, which went with them.

# The Fighting on Leyte Continues

As MacArthur's troops pushed inland from their landing beaches on Leyte, their principal resistance came from Japanese soldiers entrenched in well-camouflaged pill-boxes and coconut log bunkers. The Japanese had more than 250,000 troops stationed in the Philippines. On Leyte alone, there were between 60,000 and 70,000 Japanese troops.

Unfortunately for the Americans, miserable weather had bogged down supply vehicles and curtailed air support. The Sixth Army found itself engaged in a struggle through difficult terrain against stubborn resistance. Furthermore, the Army Air Forces were not able to build up enough strength on Leyte to stop the Japanese from sending in reinforcements to the island until early in December 1944.

The Sixth Army commander, Lieutenant General Walter Krueger, decided to accelerate the takeover of Leyte with an amphibious landing on the eastern side of the island, not far from the small coastal city of Ormoc. This landing would be conducted in conjunction with a strong push overland by his troops into the Ormoc Valley. With this operation, the Sixth Army commander hoped to secure control of both the valley and the port of Ormoc and thus force the Japanese defenders into the mountains near the western coast of the island, where they could neither escape nor be reinforced.

On the night of December 6, 1944, two different convoys were sailing toward the same location at Ormoc Bay. One contained the U.S. Army Seventy-seventh Infantry Division; the other contained Japanese reinforcements for Leyte. American pilots spotted the Japanese convoy and, in the most intense aerial battle of the entire Leyte campaign, sank four of the enemy's six transport ships on the morning of December 7. An estimated 4,000 Japanese soldiers and sailors lost their lives during this engagement.

OPPOSITE: While their clothes wave in the breeze, artillerymen of the U.S. Army Tenth Corps fire a battery of 155-mm guns, nicknamed "Long Toms," into the town of Carigara on the shore of Carigara Bay on the Philippine island of Leyte in November 1944. The Long Tom could fire a 100-pound (45kg) projectile to a maximum range of 14 miles (22.4km). BELOW: U.S. Army Mitchell B-25 medium bombers attempting to sink a Japanese transport ship straddle their target with high-explosive bombs without hitting it. In a design alteration intended to improve the effectiveness of attacks on enemy shipping in the Pacific, the "J" model featured a specially modified nose mounting eight 50-caliber machine guns.

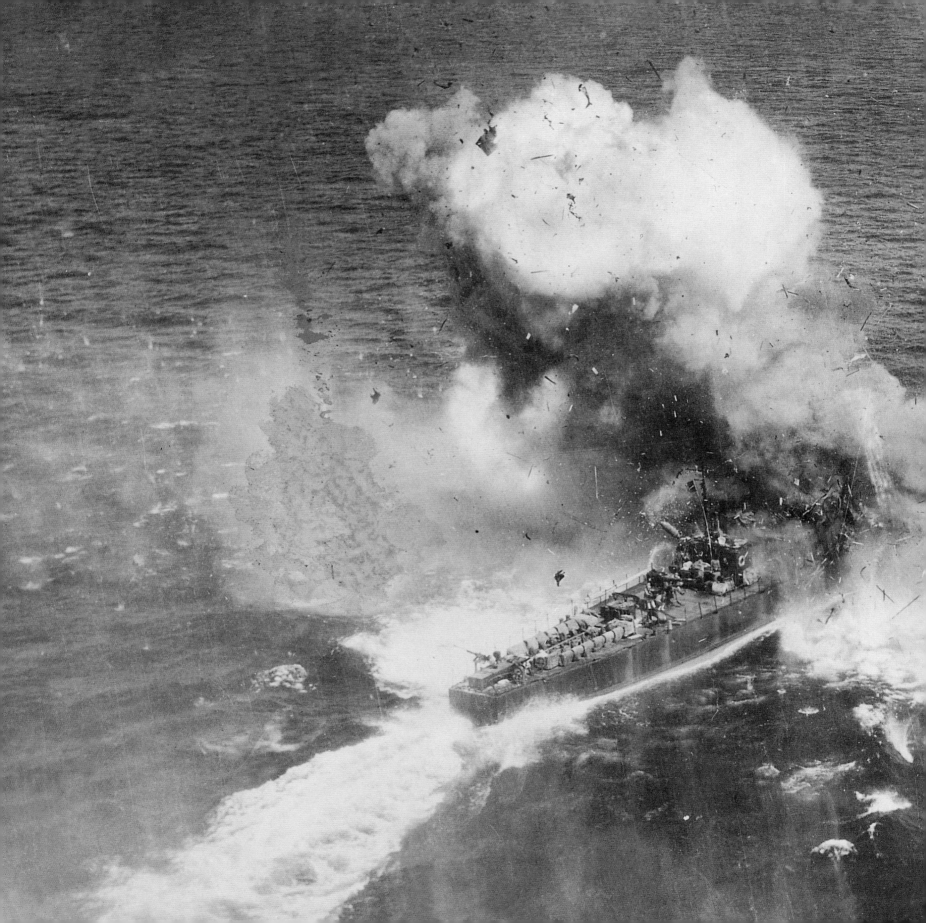

The next morning, the American Seventy-seventh Division landed on the shores of Ormoc Bay. While Japanese ground defenses offered little resistance to the American landing, the Japanese launched a fierce aerial offensive against the American ships anchored offshore. In the space of about nine hours, the Japanese flew sixteen missions against the American ships. While American planes did an excellent job of protecting the convoy, a few enemy planes broke through and successfully attacked five vessels, two of which had to be abandoned and then sunk by American naval gunfire.

On December 10, the Americans began their attack on the town of Ormoc—the largest commercial center in western Leyte; at the same time, other units were pushing into the Ormoc Valley. The capture of Ormoc and the surrounding area had an important effect on Japanese military strength on Leyte, since it cut off a port that had been used to bring in both reinforcements and supplies to the battle on the island.

In one last desperate gamble to take the initiative away from MacArthur's forces on Leyte, the Japanese launched a number of airborne attacks on American airfields in early December 1944. Japanese paratroopers, however, did only minor damage to a few American planes and some fuel and supply dumps before being killed or captured.

The Japanese had invested heavily in their efforts to hold Leyte. The Japanese Army lost four divisions and several combat units. The Navy lost twenty-six major warships and forty-six large transports and merchant ships. The battle for Leyte also reduced Japanese land-based air capability in the Philippines by over 50 percent.

After Leyte was taken, the choice of targets for the Joint Chiefs was between Luzon and Formosa. Since the Japanese had overrun the B-29 airbase sites in eastern China and the Marianas provided the B-29 bases needed for bombing Japan, the Joint Chiefs selected Luzon. MacArthur decreed that his forces could start invading Luzon from Leyte in late December 1944— three months before Nimitz would have been able to invade Formosa.

A Japanese Navy destroyer escort explodes in a cloud of debris and smoke after being hit dead center by a bomb from a U.S. Army B-25 Mitchell medium bomber. The Japanese warship was escorting a convoy of troop transports to the island of Leyte's Ormoc Bay in the Philippines in early November 1944.

With his eyes closed, one of MacArthur's soldiers prepares to fire an M1A1 2.36-inch (6cm) rocket launcher (bazooka) at a Japanese target on the Philippine island of Luzon. Though the bazooka was originally designed strictly as an antitank weapon, American soldiers soon discovered that the weapon was also very effective against defensive fortifications.

# The Invasion of Luzon

The first step in the plan to invade Luzon was the seizure of the southwest corner of Mindoro Island, located 150 miles (241km) south of Manila, on December 15, 1944. The object of this move was to conquer more air bases from which to support operations on Luzon. After making feints at southern Luzon to mislead the Japanese as to their real point of attack, MacArthur's forces invaded Luzon itself on January 9, 1945, landing along the shores of the Lingayen Gulf. The American soldiers met with little opposition as they pushed inland, since the Japanese commander on Luzon had decided to concentrate most of his forces in the island's more easily defended mountainous regions.

Immediately after his forces landed on Luzon, MacArthur started planning for the recapture of Manila. The general's strong belief that Manila was his for the taking came from his intelligence chief, Major General Charles A. Willoughby, who had told him that the capital city of the Philippines was undefended. MacArthur's staff had already made plans for a massive victory parade through the city. What the supreme commander did not know was that, against the wishes of the Japanese Army commander on Luzon, a Japanese rear admiral inside Manila, Denshichi Okochi, had decided to defend the city on his own initiative. Roughly 20,000 men were under his command.

By the end of the first week of February, MacArthur had three divisions poised in the suburbs of Manila. As the soldiers under MacArthur's command continued their drive toward the center of the city, Japanese resistance became progressively stronger. Although American soldiers relied heavily on artillery, tanks, tank destroyers, mortar, and bazooka fire for all advances, the bloody job of clearing individual buildings often fell to small groups of infantrymen.

As a grenade explodes in a Japanese dugout, U.S. troops stand ready to fire at any enemy soldiers who attempt to escape. The standard infantry rifle used by both the U.S. Army and Marine Corps during the fighting in the Pacific was the .30-caliber M1 Garand. First introduced into Army service in 1937, the Garand was a semiautomatic, gas-operated weapon with an internal eight-round magazine.

# Kamikaze

Unable to inflict serious losses on the U.S. Navy Pacific Fleet, and facing a desperate situation, the Japanese recruited volunteer pilots who were willing to fly their explosive-laden aircraft on one-way suicide attack missions against U.S. Navy warships. The Japanese called these pilots *kamikaze*. The term *kamikaze* means "divine wind," and refers to the fortuitous typhoon in the thirteenth century that destroyed the great Mongol invasion fleet set on conquering Japan.

The first kamikaze units went into action during the three-day naval battle of Leyte Gulf in late October 1944. They sank one U.S. Navy escort carrier and badly damaged two others. By January 1945, when the Japanese ran out of aircraft in the Philippines, they had managed to sink sixteen U.S. Navy ships and to damage another eighty-six, including five battleships, twenty-two aircraft carriers, and twenty-eight destroyers or destroyer escorts.

The senior leadership of the U.S. Navy hoped that the kamikaze attacks in the Philippines had been strictly a local phenomenon. They did not know that the Japanese were already massing up to 10,000 additional kamikaze planes in an effort to stop the planned U.S. Navy invasion of Okinawa in April 1945.

Firing fast and furiously, the gun crew of a quadruple 40-mm "Bofors" anti-aircraft gun vainly attempts to destroy approaching Japanese kamikaze planes before they get too close. The 40-mm Bofors gun could accurately fire a 2-pound (0.9kg) high-explosive shell to a range of 5,000 yards (4,560m) or up to a height of 14,000 feet (4,256m). Shells were manually loaded into the weapon in four-round clips fed from the top of the gun's breech. The rate of fire of each gun tube was 160 rounds per minute. The weapon was well-liked by gun crews for its high rate of fire, hitting power, and reliability.

Japanese *kamikaze* planes struck the U.S. Navy aircraft carrier *Bunker Hill* near Japan on the morning of May 11, 1945. The resulting explosions and fires almost destroyed the ship. Here, smoke rises from the 20-mm anti-aircraft guns and the wrecked flight deck.

The old walled city of Intramuros was the last Japanese stronghold in Manila. Originally located on the edge of Manila Bay, Intramuros was bordered on three sides by an old moat and had been converted into a public park and golf course. In the center of Intramuros was an old Spanish stone fort built in 1590. Knowing that the Japanese had built an elaborate tunnel system under the old walled city, which allowed troop movement and shelter from American shellfire, MacArthur's field commanders launched two simultaneous assaults on Intramuros from different directions. This confused the Japanese and also forced them to divide their forces in response.

By March 3, all organized resistance in Manila had ceased. Unfortunately, the citizens of Manila paid a very heavy price for their freedom from Japanese occupation. Almost 100,000 Filipinos died before the last Japanese defensive position in Manila had been overrun. American casualties included only 1,010 dead and 6,575 wounded. Estimated Japanese casualties included 17,000 dead. Another 3,000 soldiers took refuge in the mountains surrounding Manila.

LEFT: Smoke resulting from bombs dropped by U.S. Navy planes rises from the Japanese-occupied city of Manila in the Philippines on December 12, 1944. The objective of the aerial attack was to destroy shipping docks, warehouses, and other waterfront installations in use by the Japanese Navy.
ABOVE: An American soldier carries a shell-shocked Philippine woman to a first-aid station after the destruction of the building in which she and her family had sought shelter. During the fierce fighting between U.S. and Japanese troops in Manila, untold thousands of the city's inhabitants were killed or wounded.

OPPOSITE: U.S. paratroopers drift down out of the sky to land on the Japanese-defended island of Corregidor on the morning of February 16, 1945. To secure the island, MacArthur employed one of the most difficult modern military maneuvers—a coordinated parachute and amphibious attack. His decision had a lot to do with what happened to the Japanese amphibious assault on the island in May 1942, when the landing forces took heavy losses in both troops and equipment.
LEFT: Corregidor from the sky, shortly after the island was declared secure on February 27, 1945. The bombed-out buildings on the right are prewar concrete barracks inhabited by U.S. soldiers before the Japanese conquest of the Philippines. The entire island is still covered with the white silk parachutes of the 503rd Airborne Regiment.

## The Capture of Corregidor

As Manila was being "liberated" from the Japanese, MacArthur turned his attention to the recapture of Bataan and the island of Corregidor so that naval support ships could safely use Manila Bay. Since the Japanese commander on Luzon had already decided that trying to defend Bataan made no tactical sense, MacArthur's forces met little resistance when they landed on Bataan. Unfortunately, the recapture of the island of Corregidor proved to be a much tougher job for MacArthur's troops.

As a prelude to the landing on Corregidor, the island had been pounded steadily from the sea and air since the last week of January 1945.

As a result of faulty intelligence work, MacArthur was led to believe that there were only 900 Japanese troops stationed on the island of Corregidor. In reality, there were almost 5,000 Japanese soldiers prepared to die defending the island. The assault on Corregidor began when 1,000 paratroopers from the 503rd Airborne Regiment landed on the western half of the island on the morning of February 16. The Japanese defenders were taken by surprise and failed to inflict any casualties on the Americans.

An hour after the paratroopers were dropped on Corregidor, a second group of 1,000 soldiers from the Thirty-fourth Regimental Combat Team were brought in by boat. This assault also caught the Japanese defenders by surprise. The Japanese eventually reacted to the seaborne assault and made later landings very costly for MacArthur's men.

The next afternoon, 1,000 additional soldiers were air-dropped on Corregidor. This time the element of surprise was gone. The Japanese defenders on Corregidor were ready and waiting. Japanese fire caused heavy losses among the second wave of parachutists of the 503rd Airborne. A third airborne assault planned for Corregidor on the same day was canceled due to the very high casualty rate. Instead, these troops were landed on the island by boat on February 17.

On February 27, eleven days after the invasion had started, Corregidor was declared secure. MacArthur's

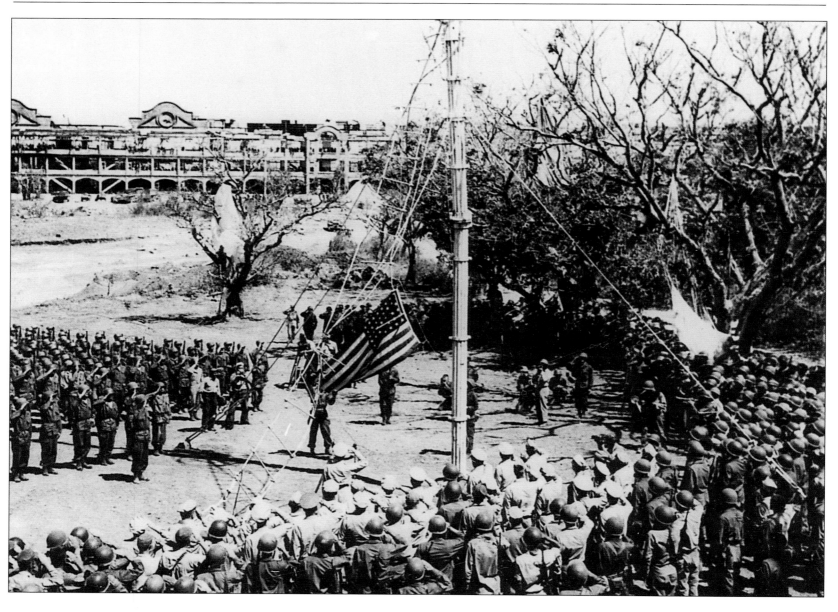

MacArthur returned to his former headquarters on Corregidor on March 2, 1945. In a dramatic ceremony, the commander of the 503rd Airborne Regiment presented the captured island to his chief. After awarding the unit commander a Distinguished Service Cross, MacArthur ordered the American flag raised over Corregidor again.

forces counted 4,500 dead Japanese soldiers on the island. Only twenty Japanese soldiers were captured. The rest of the Japanese defenders were either buried in the tunnels under the island or had managed to escape the island during the fighting.

The Japanese surrender of Corregidor was more than just a minor tactical victory for MacArthur; it was the fulfillment of a personal crusade that had started with the loss of the island to the Japanese three years before. On March 2, 1945, General Douglas A.

MacArthur and many members of his prewar staff attended an emotional ceremony on Corregidor for the raising of the American flag over the small, battle-scarred island.

The capture of the island of Corregidor, important as it was, did not completely secure Manila Bay. Japanese troops still occupied the southern shore of the bay, as well as many of the small islands located between Corregidor and Luzon. More fighting remained before the Philippines could be liberated.

# Mopping Up Luzon

Despite the capture of the Philippine capital city of Manila, the Bataan Peninsula, and the island of Corregidor, fighting for the island of Luzon continued. The Japanese commander on the island had gathered elements of his remaining forces in the mountains of southern Luzon. These enemy forces would remain a threat to the recently liberated city of Manila because they were in position to destroy the dams that supplied water to the city. They were also positioned to attack American soldiers situated near Manila.

On March 5, 1945, MacArthur ordered his First Cavalry and Sixth Infantry Divisions to capture the areas around the dams. On March 8, after a heavy, two-day aerial bombardment of the objective, MacArthur deployed his forces. Japanese resistance was fierce, and U.S. progress was slow. It would take U.S. forces until the middle of June 1945 to clear most of the Japanese defenders out of the mountains of southern Luzon. While some of his forces were busy with that task, an even bigger battle was raging in the northern mountains of Luzon. It was here that the Japanese had stationed the major portion of their ground forces. The struggle to capture the island's northern mountains spanned more than four months—beginning in mid-February and winding up near the end of June.

A Japanese cruiser in the Philippines frantically maneuvers to avoid bombs from a U.S. Navy carrier aircraft. The ship was finally hit a few minutes after this photograph was taken, and it eventually sank. The sea battles that raged around the Philippines in late 1944 broke the back of the Japanese Navy. It would not pose a serious threat to the U.S. Navy for the remainder of the war.

U.S. soldiers on the main Philippine island of Luzon take cover behind a short fence. At left is an air-cooled Browning M1919A4 .30-caliber machine gun, which had a rate of fire of 400 to 500 rounds per minute. At far right, a soldier holds a .30-caliber Browning automatic rifle, commonly referred to by its initials, "BAR." The BAR weighed about 16 pounds (7.2kg) and fired from an external twenty-round box magazine.

# Cleaning Up the Philippines

While the battle for Luzon was raging, MacArthur sent elements of his command to capture some of the strategically situated islands of the southern Philippines and the island of Borneo in the former Dutch East Indies. On April 21, 1945, MacArthur had issued a communiqué describing the significance of these operations, including this excerpt:

*In addition to the main islands of Leyte, Samara, Mindoro, Pane, Paladin, Negros, Bohol and Masbate, Japanese garrisons on a score of lesser islands . . . have been eliminated. This sweep clears the center of the Philippines and leaves the only remaining enemy organized resistance in Mindanao on the south and upper Luzon on the north.*

MacArthur's forces invaded the island of Mindanao on April 17, 1945. Organized Japanese resistance on the island lasted until June 30. It took until mid-August, however, to round up the last Japanese stragglers hiding in the island's mountains.

In a special communiqué to the press on July 5, 1945, MacArthur announced:

*The entire Philippine Islands are now liberated, and the Philippine Campaign can be regarded as virtually closed. Some minor isolated action of a guerrilla nature in the practically uninhabited mountain ranges may occasionally persist but this great landmass of 115,600 square miles [186,000 sq. km] with a population of 17,000,000 is now freed of the invader. The enemy during the operations employed twenty-three divisions, all of which were practically annihilated. Our forces comprised seventeen divisions. This was one of the rare instances when in a long campaign a ground force superior in numbers was entirely destroyed by a numerically inferior opponent.*

# Chapter 6

# The Final Battles

THE AMPHIBIOUS OPERATIONS UNDERTAKEN IN THE CENTRAL PACIFIC BY FORCES
under the command of Admiral Nimitz began in late 1943 and continued through 1944. Their
successes carried American soldiers and sailors to the very doorstep of the Japanese Empire.

The occupation of Saipan, Tinian, and Guam in the Mariana Islands had established bases
from which long-range B-29 bombers could strike the main industrial centers of Japan. However,
to provide the bombers with fighter escort protection, the island of Iwo Jima—located 300 miles
(480 km) northwest of the Mariana Islands and roughly 750 miles (1,200km) south of Tokyo—
had to be captured.

Important advantages to be gained from the capture of Iwo Jima included the following: there
were three existing Japanese-built airfields that could be used by American planes; its capture
would deprive the Japanese of an important early warning site
for American bomber raids on Japan; and the island would provide a safe landing site for damaged B-29s that might otherwise
be forced to ditch in the sea.

Iwo Jima, though small, is the largest island in the Volcano
Island group. It is less than 5 miles (8km) long and between
0.5 mile (0.8km) and 2.5 miles (4km) wide. The 556-foot
(169m) dormant volcano Mount Suribachi dominates the narrow
southern end of the island and overlooks the only beaches prac-
tical for landing troops. The broken and convoluted terrain on
the northern end of Iwo Jima is dotted with steam vents and
caves, making it a defender's dream. More than one Marine
who survived the assault on Iwo Jima compared the island to
Dante's Inferno.

LEFT: Hundreds of high-explosive
bombs rain down on the docks
of a Japanese city, as thick clouds
of smoke rise up from targets
already struck by bombs. The
first B-29 raid on the Japanese
home islands occurred on June
14, 1944, and consisted of sixty-
three aircraft. The U.S. commander of the B-29 unit that made
the raid declared that the attack
was "but the beginning of the
organized destruction of the
Japanese industrial empire."

The destroyed remains of a single Marine Corps M-4 Sherman tank and two amphibious tractors littering one of the beaches on Iwo Jima attest to the ferocity of the fighting on the island. The first obstacle encountered by the Marines landing on the island on February 19, 1945, was not the Japanese but the beaches themselves. Iwo Jima was an emerging volcano; its steep beaches dropped off sharply, producing a narrow but violent surf zone. The soft black sand immobilized both wheeled and tracked vehicles.

Senior American military leaders anticipated that Japanese resistance on Iwo Jima would be severe because of the terrain and the fact that the Japanese had time to heavily fortify the island. The attack plan called for a landing force of 60,000 Marines to be put ashore by a naval force of more than 800 ships manned by approximately 220,000 naval personnel. American intelligence experts had estimated that the Japanese had 12,000 to 13,000 troops on Iwo Jima. Unfortunately for the Americans, Japanese forces proved to be almost twice that size—almost 23,000 men.

For seven months prior to the planned February 1945 assault on Iwo Jima, the island was subjected to air attacks and surface bombardments, which increased in frequency and intensity from December 1944 onward. On February 16, the pre-invasion bombardment of Iwo Jima began. After three days of naval and aerial bombardment, the Fourth and Fifth Marine Divisions began landing on the southeast shore of Iwo Jima. Initial Japanese opposition consisted of light mortar and artillery fire. Resistance rapidly developed in intensity during the day, with a devastating curtain of artillery, rocket, and mortar fire on the beaches. The Marines inched ahead against determined resistance from heavily fortified Japanese positions.

The Marines who came ashore on Iwo Jima on February 19, 1945, encountered an intricate system of defenses. The defending garrison was deployed in an interlocking system of caves, pillboxes, and blockhouses. Guns on Mount Suribachi at the southern tip of the island and in elevated positions on the rest of the island were able to fire on the Marines before and after they landed.

By the end of the first day, despite heavy losses in personnel, the Marines had advanced across the width of the island at its narrow southwestern tip. Possession of this strip of land isolated the Japanese troops on Mount Suribachi from the main Japanese force in the north.

During the early morning hours of February 20, the Marines broke up a strong Japanese counterattack. By the end of the day, the Marines had captured one of the three enemy airfields on the island.

ABOVE: Expended shells and open ammunition boxes testify to the heavy supporting fire that this water-cooled Browning M1917A1 .30-caliber machine gun poured on the Japanese defensive positions as the U.S. Marines advanced across the island. LEFT: On Iwo Jima, wounded Marines are helped to a first-aid station. U.S. Navy personnel provided medical support, in the form of one medic for every Marine squad of thirteen men, throughout the war. Some wounded Marines received treatment in a field hospital tent, recuperated in a bunker, and were returned to the front line only to receive a second or third wound.

One of the most famous pictures to come out of the war in the Pacific was this image of five U.S. Marines and a U.S. Navy corpsman raising an American flag on Mount Suribachi on February 23, 1945. The picture was taken by Joe Rosenthal, an Associated Press photographer who accompanied the group to the peak.

Intense fighting continued during the third day of the invasion. Reserve troops of the Third Marine Division landed and moved into line between the Fourth and Fifth Divisions. Although Japanese air strength was generally light, air attacks successfully sank a U.S. Navy escort carrier. During the night, the Japanese launched numerous counterattacks, but they were thrown back each time.

The following morning, the Marines renewed the attack; by noon, they were advancing slowly under adverse weather conditions, knocking out enemy strongholds as they went. During the afternoon, the Japanese counterattacked again, exerting maximum pressure on both flanks of the Marine spearhead, which was headed for another Japanese airfield. These counterattacks were beaten back with heavy losses to the Japanese.

Part of the second Japanese airfield was occupied on February 23, while other Marines stormed the steep slopes of Mount Suribachi and captured the summit, along with the Japanese gun positions that had dominated the island. At 10:35 A.M., members of the Twenty-eighth Marine Regiment hoisted the U.S. flag over the extinct volcano.

By February 25, Marines of all three divisions, spearheaded by tanks, had captured approximately half the island, including the remainder of the second Japanese airfield, and were closing in on the main village of Iwo Jima. The advance was made against fanatical resistance—rockets, bazooka-type guns, and smaller guns blazed from pillboxes.

By the end of February, Marine Corps observation and artillery spotting planes were operating from the first Japanese airfield. The Third and Fourth Marine Divisions had captured hills that further reduced the enemy's firepower and freed the beaches for safe landing of supplies. Despite heavy losses, the Japanese continued to resist, but the Marines were established on high ground, and the conquest of Iwo Jima was assured.

Fierce ground fighting on Iwo Jima was still in progress on the first day of March. By nightfall on March 2, however, the Marines had captured the remaining airfield on Iwo Jima. Surviving Japanese troops were confined to an area fringing the northeastern end of the island.

The B-29 four-engine bombers that pounded the home islands of Japan from July 1944 till the end of the war evolved from an Army Air Corps (renamed the U.S. Army Air Forces after the attack on Pearl Harbor) requirement first set in 1940. What the Air Corps wanted was a long-range heavy bomber able to carry a 2,000-pound (906kg) payload of bombs at 400 miles per hour (640kph) to a range of 5,333 miles (8,533km). The prototype of the B-29 bomber first flew successfully in September 1942. The first production examples of the bomber appeared in late 1943.

The first captured Japanese airfield had been in use for a few days by Marine light artillery spotting planes. On March 3, it proved its worth when a B-29 made a successful emergency landing at Iwo Jima after a strike against the Japanese mainland. More such landings soon followed as U.S. troops stepped up the tempo of air strikes against Japan. On March 6, the first land-based fighter planes arrived, made patrol flights the following day, and were relieving carrier aircraft in close support of troops by the third day. The second Japanese airfield became operational on March 16—the same day that organized Japanese resistance was declared at an end.

The capture of the island had come after twenty-six days of actual combat; almost all of the 24,000 defending Japanese troops had died. American casualties ashore amounted to 20,196, with 4,305 killed in action. The heavy losses among the Marines at Iwo Jima were somewhat offset by the fact that 2,251 B-29s were subsequently able to make forced landings on the island. Without Iwo Jima as an emergency landing field, 24,761 flight crewmen might have died as their planes crashed into the sea.

## The Invasion of Okinawa

After Iwo Jima, the next step toward Japan was the island of Okinawa—the largest island in the Ryukyu Island chain. Okinawa is sixty miles (97km) long and between two miles (3km) and eighteen miles (29km) wide, with an area of 485 square miles (780 sq. km). The Ryukyu Islands extend in a shallow loop from Kyushu (the southernmost of the main Japanese islands) to Japanese-held Formosa (now known as Taiwan).

Okinawa offered numerous sites for airfields from which almost any type of aircraft could reach the industrial heart of Japan, the Chinese mainland, and the Indo-China and Singapore areas. Okinawa also contained several excellent areas to anchor large numbers of ships in relative safety.

From many standpoints, the invasion of Okinawa was the most difficult ever undertaken by American forces in the Pacific. The Japanese had anticipated the American invasion and were prepared with an impressive array of defensive fortifications, including more than 96 miles (154km) of underground tunnels. About

76,000 Japanese troops, backed up by tanks and artillery, were ready to defend the island to the death. An additional 24,000 men in militia and labor groups supported the troops.

The most serious threat to the planned American invasion of Okinawa was its proximity to Japan. Japanese air and navy forces could attack Okinawa just as easily as the Americans could attack Japan. While the Japanese Navy was greatly reduced in numbers and effectiveness, it could still mount hit-and-run raids on the American naval forces arrayed around Okinawa. Air attack, particularly in the form of suicide runs, was the greatest menace. Japanese airfields within easy attack range of Okinawa were too numerous and heavily defended for decisive American air strikes.

Preceded by an intense naval and air bombardment, the American Tenth Army (composed of both U.S. Army and Marine Corps divisions) landed on the beaches of Okinawa according to schedule on the morning of April 1. Encountering only weak resistance from the

ABOVE: Early on the morning of April 1, 1945, troops from the U.S. Army and Marine Corps commenced landing on the western beaches of the island of Okinawa. This event marked the final great amphibious operation of the war. Here, the leading elements of the Third Marine Amphibious Corps come ashore on Okinawa. LEFT: On Okinawa, a short-range Japanese flying bomb was captured intact. These one-man suicide aircraft were packed with more than a ton of high explosives. They were carried into battle underneath modified twin-engine bombers. Once in sight of a target, they were released. The pilot then fired the three rear-mounted rocket engines and aimed himself and his aircraft at a selected target.

A U.S. Marine on Okinawa aims his M1 "Thompson" submachine gun at approaching Japanese soldiers. The weapon, which entered American military service in the 1920s, weighed about 10 pounds (4.5kg) and could be fired from a detachable box magazine carrying either twenty or thirty rounds. Early models could also be fired from a fifty-round drum magazine. Firing a low-power .45-caliber round, the Thompson was most effective at very close ranges or in confined spaces.

## Zippo Tanks

**During the battle for Okinawa, one of the most useful vehicles in the Marine Corps inventory was the flame-throwing tank nicknamed the "Zippo." The Zippo consisted of an M-4 Sherman medium tank with its turret-mounted 75-mm main gun removed and replaced with a Mark I flamethrower. Using napalm-thickened fuel, the Zippo tanks had a range up to 150 yards (137 m). The Japanese soldiers so feared these tanks that they formed special suicide squads to destroy them. To protect their valuable flame-throwing tanks, the Marines always sent them into battle with covering forces.**

defenders, U.S. assault troops moved rapidly inland and soon captured two Japanese-built airfields with light losses. By the end of the first day, the Tenth Army, with approximately 50,000 troops ashore, had gained a beachhead 4,000 yards (3,658m) to 5,000 yards (4,572m) deep. Proceeding rapidly against initially light Japanese defenses, American troops crossed the island to its eastern shore.

The Japanese had made no serious attempt to stop the American invasion forces at the beaches. As the attack progressed, it became evident that they had withdrawn most of their forces to the southernmost part of the island, where they could establish their defenses in depth on terrain ideal for defense and delaying-action tactics. The Japanese defenses consisted of blockhouses, pillboxes, and caves protected by double-apron barbed wire and minefields.

In the north, progress was rapid against scattered opposition. By April 22, all organized resistance in the northern two-thirds of the island had ceased, leaving the American soldiers with only patrolling and mopping-up activities. Japanese soldiers stubbornly contested the American advance in the south. From April 4 to May 26,

American lines advanced only about 4 miles (6.4km). It took from May 26 to June 21 to cover the remaining 10 miles (16km) to the southern tip of the island.

An example of the fierce fighting on Okinawa comes from the Medal of Honor citation of U.S. Army Sergeant John Meagher won on June 19:

*In the heat of the fight, he mounted an assault tank, and, with bullets splattering about him, designated targets to the gunner. Seeing an enemy soldier carrying an explosive charge dash for the tank treads, he shouted fire orders to the gunner, leaped from the tank, and bayoneted the charging soldier. Knocked unconscious and his rifle destroyed, he regained consciousness, secured a machine gun from the tank, and began a furious one-man assault on the enemy. Firing from the hip, moving through vicious crossfire that ripped through his clothing, he charged the nearest pill-box, killing six. Going on amid the hail of bullets and grenades, he dashed for a second enemy gun, running out of ammunition just as he reached the position. He grasped his empty gun by the barrel and in a violent onslaught killed the crew.*

A U.S. Navy battleship fires its forward 16-inch (40cm) guns in support of ground troops. A high-ranking U.S. Navy officer wrote: "There can be little doubt that naval gunfire is the most feared and most effective of all weapons with which the Japanese are confronted in resisting a landing and assault."

The Japanese *kamikaze* attacks on the U.S. Navy during the last months of the war in the Pacific took a heavy toll on men and ships. The most important target of the Japanese suicide pilots was always the Navy's aircraft carriers. Unlike other large warships that had armored top decks, such as battleships or cruisers, U.S. aircraft carriers had wooden flight decks supported by non-armored steel bracing. As can be seen in this picture, the impact of a *kamikaze* could have terrible results on a carrier.

On June 21, after eighty-two days of bitter fighting, organized resistance was declared ended, even though two small pockets of Japanese soldiers continued resisting until the end of the month.

American personnel losses in the conquest of Okinawa were the highest of the war, with a total of 72,000 casualties, including 6,139 dead. Japanese losses, including labor groups and local militia, were estimated at 92,398 men. Of the 7,600 enemy personnel who surrendered to American forces on Okinawa, most were laborers or militia personnel.

A Japanese torpedo plane, seen from a U.S. Navy ship, flies through an intense hail of anti-aircraft fire to deliver its payload. Flying a torpedo plane in any navy during World War II was an extremely dangerous job—the pilot had to fly a slow, low-level, and fairly straight approach to his target, making him an easy target for the defending ship's weapons.

## Suicide Missions

Taking advantage of the suicidal determination of their troops on Okinawa, the Japanese launched a series of massive kamikaze raids against the U.S. Navy ships near the island. The first occurred on March 24. The first real damage was done on March 26, and by June 21, when Japanese resistance on the island had ceased, about 250 U.S. Navy vessels of all types had been severely damaged by kamikaze attacks. Thirty-four ships and 763 aircraft were totally destroyed. Losses among naval personnel were also high, with more than 5,000 killed

# The Death of the Battleship *Yamato*

In one last desperate attempt to push U.S. forces off the island of Okinawa in early April 1945, the Japanese military high command decided to launch a combined aerial and naval assault on the large U.S. Navy invasion fleet in the waters around Okinawa. The naval element of the attacking Japanese force consisted of the super battleship *Yamato*, one cruiser, and eight destroyers. Their job was to attract as many U.S. carrier planes as they could from the skies around the island, thus allowing a massive *kamikaze* raid to strike at the unprotected American troop and support ships.

Due to Japan's fuel shortage, the *Yamato* and its supporting ships were strictly on a one-way mission, and the ship's officers had no illusions about the eventual outcome of the operation. The Japanese military high command had made no efforts to provide air cover for the *Yamato* and its supporting ships as they reached the waters around

Okinawa. The Japanese Navy General Staff had opposed the operation from the start, believing that it was inhuman to order what was left of the once-proud fleet to carry out such a suicidal mission. Their objections were overruled.

The *Yamato* and its supporting ships sailed from southern Japan during the early morning hours of April 6, 1945. They were soon spotted by U.S. bombers and submarines, which reported the ships' positions to headquarters. During that night and in the early morning darkness of April 7, a U.S. submarine tailed the Japanese ships, constantly reporting their locations. A plane from the U.S. aircraft carrier *Essex* picked up their trail the following morning. The U.S. Navy quickly assembled a force of more than 380 torpedo planes and dive-bombers to attack the

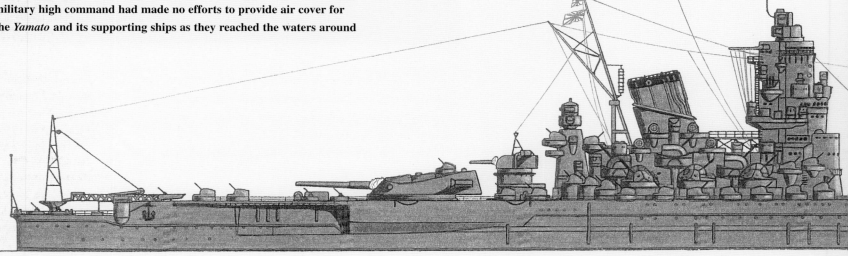

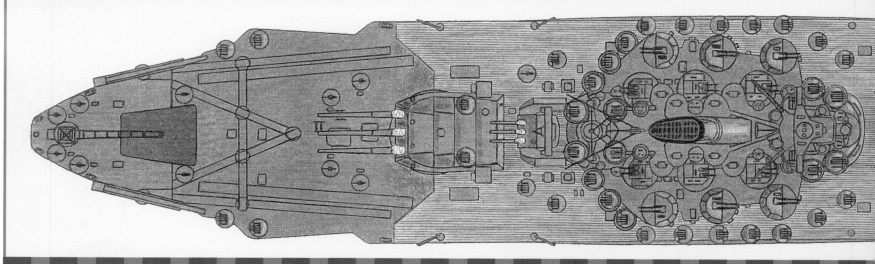

enemy ships, with the most important target being the *Yamato*.

The first U.S. aerial attack on the Japanese ships began at 12:32 p.m. The *Yamato* and the other Japanese ships opened fire with every weapon they had. Undeterred by the heavy anti-aircraft fire, the U.S. pilots pressed their attacks. The first bomb struck the *Yamato* at 12:40 p.m. Ten minutes later, the first of more than sixteen U.S. torpedoes punched a hole in the ship's hull. By 2:23 p.m., the *Yamato* could take no more punishment, and it slid under the waves with most of its crew. In addition to the *Yamato*, the U.S. pilots also sank the single supporting cruiser and four of the eight destroyers assigned to protect the battleship.

The massive *kamikaze* attack that was to sink the U.S. invasion fleet off Okinawa as the *Yamato* distracted the fleet's carrier planes inflicted little serious damage.

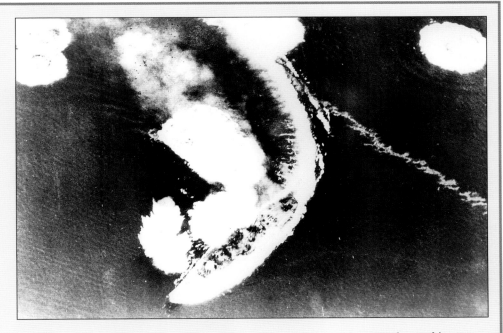

I.M.S. *Yamato*

1944–1945

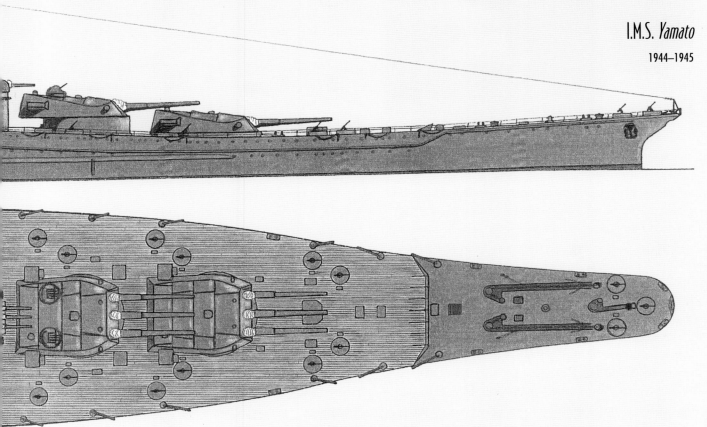

ABOVE: The powerful Japanese super battleship *Yamato* suffers a near miss from a bomb delivered by a U.S. Navy dive-bomber. LEFT: The Japanese battleship *Yamato*, seen here in overhead and side views, and its sister ship, the *Musashi*, were the most powerful ships of their type to see service in World War II. Construction on both ships began in 1937. The *Yamato* entered service a week after the attack on Pearl Harbor. Main armament of the ships consisted of nine massive 18-inch (45cm) guns mounted in three triple-armored turrets. A third ship in the same class, the *Shinano*, was completed as an aircraft carrier during the war years to compensate for the shortage of such vessels in the Japanese Navy. All three ships were lost in action during the war.

A massive mushroom cloud rises above the Japanese city of Nagasaki on August 9, 1945, following the explosion of an atomic bomb dropped from a specially modified B-29 bomber. Nagasaki was the second Japanese city to suffer the ravages of an atomic bomb blast. Hiroshima was bombed three days before Nagasaki, and was approximately 60 percent destroyed. The combined effects of these two atomic bomb blasts helped push Japanese leaders into peace talks.

12:30 P.M. By 2:23 P.M., the ship slid under the waves after suffering dozens of bomb and torpedo hits. Of the 2,400 Japanese sailors on the ship, only 269 survived.

## The End of the War

On May 25, 1945, the Joint Chiefs of Staff assigned General MacArthur the job of laying the groundwork for the invasion of Japan. A target date of November 1, 1945, was set for the invasion of Kyushu, the southern-most Japanese home island. Admiral Nimitz was given the responsibility for all naval operations in and around Japan, including the amphibious landing forces.

By the summer of 1945, it was obvious to many high-ranking military and civilian leaders in Japan that the end of the war was near. U.S. Navy submarines had sunk a substantial proportion of Japan's merchant marine fleet, effectively cutting Japan off from the natural resources it needed to continue the war. The planes and warships that remained had used up the last of the fuel reserves. American air raids on Japan had destroyed many of its major cities, and the raids were increasing in severity.

As MacArthur pushed ahead with his plans for the invasion of Japan, negotiations were under way that ultimately would make an invasion unnecessary. On July 26, 1945, President Harry Truman issued an ultimatum to the Japanese government that gave Japan the choice of surrender or destruction.

Japan rejected Truman's ultimatum, and on August 6, 1945, a single B-29 dropped an atomic bomb on the Japanese port city of Hiroshima.

On August 9, the Soviet Union entered the war against Japan, attacking Japanese forces in Manchuria; on the same day, another B-29 dropped a second atomic bomb on the Japanese city of Nagasaki. On August 10, stunned by the unprecedented destruction and loss of life wrought by the A-bomb, Japan surrendered.

While the Japanese government negotiated final surrender terms, the Joint Chiefs completed plans for the occupation of Japan. Arrangements for the hoped-for peaceful entry of Allied forces into Japan were based on the actual invasion plans. The immediate objective of the Allied occupation of Japan was the disarming and

and another 5,000 wounded. The Japanese lost 7,830 aircraft in their effort to sink the American fleet.

As an extension of the air battle over Okinawa, the Japanese Navy mounted its only real surface threat to the success of the American invasion. Japan sent the battleship *Yamato* (the largest in the world) and a supporting force of one cruiser and eight destroyers on a suicide mission to destroy the American transport ships around Okinawa. Because there would be no air cover for the Japanese ships, this mission was doomed from the beginning.

American submarines sighted the *Yamato* and its supporting ships on April 6, only two hours after the massive ship left Japan. A plane from the American aircraft carrier *Essex* picked up the trail the next morning. The U.S. Navy quickly assembled a force of more than 380 torpedo and dive-bombers to attack the enemy battleship. The first American aerial attack began at

# The Atomic Bomb

The development of the atomic bomb began in 1939 when a small group of eminent scientists in the United States called the American government's attention to the vast potential of atomic energy for military purposes. Alarmed by the facts presented by this group, and by the warning that Germany was already carrying out experiments in the field, the U.S. government began a very secret program in October of that year. Initially, the program began with a very modest appropriation, but before long it was expanded into the two-billion-dollar Manhattan Project.

At the end of 1944, in anticipation of having an atomic bomb ready for testing by the summer of 1945, the senior leaders of the American military began compiling a list of possible Japanese targets. A special B-29 bomber squadron was organized and trained for the job of delivering atomic bombs to targets in Japan.

On July 16, 1945, the first atomic bomb was successfully exploded in a spectacular demonstration at Alamogordo, New Mexico. Once informed of the test results, British Prime Minster Winston Churchill became convinced that the war could be concluded "in one or two violent shocks."

On July 25, President Harry S. Truman, convinced by his military advisors that an invasion of the Japanese home island would result in the loss of more than 500,000 American soldiers, decided that the best course of action, the swiftest way to end the war, was to use the bomb. The original plans called for the first atomic bomb to be dropped on Japan on August 4, but this attack had to be deferred due to bad weather. On August 5, the forecast was more favorable, and the mission was ordered for the next day.

On the morning of August 6, three B-29 bombers appeared over Hiroshima, the eighth largest city in Japan. The lead bomber, nicknamed the Enola Gay,

carried a single atomic bomb in its specially modified bomb bay. At 8:15 a.m., the bomb bay doors opened and the bomb was released. Forty-five seconds later, it exploded in a blinding flash, killing more than 100,000 people instantly; thousands more would later die of wounds and radiation poisoning. Another bomb dropped on the city of Nagasaki two days later killed only 35,000 people, but the point was made. The damage wrought by the Americans' new weapons enabled the Japanese emperor and his supporters to convince the more die-hard elements within the military that there was no use continuing the war.

The destruction inflicted by the dropping of the first atomic bomb on Hiroshima, Japan's eighth largest city, was terrible. When the bomb exploded over the city at an altitude of 800 feet (244m), more than 100,000 people died instantly. Thousands more would later perish from burns, shock, and radiation poisoning. About five square miles (13 km²) of the city were completely devastated.

demobilization of Japanese armed forces. Another objective was the occupation of major strategic areas such as seaports and airfields.

It was decided that final authority for the execution of the terms of surrender and for the occupation of Japan would rest with a supreme commander for the Allied Powers. The British, Soviet, and Chinese governments concurred with President Truman's proposal that MacArthur be be appointed to this post and be given responsibility for the overall administration of the surrender.

On August 15, 1945, Japan sent its Notification of Final Surrender to the United States. Two weeks later, Admiral Halsey's Third Fleet sailed into Tokyo Bay to prepare for the first seaborne landing on the Japanese mainland. By the next evening, there were roughly 4,200 combat-equipped soldiers of the Eleventh Airborne Division in Japan. On September 1, 1945, MacArthur joined them.

In Tokyo Bay aboard the U.S. Navy battleship *Missouri*, on the morning of September 2, 1945, Japan formally surrendered to the Allies, bringing to an end the most destructive and costly war in human history.

*Re - the war ended on Aug. 15th*

OPPOSITE: The formal surrender of Japan took place on the main deck of the U.S. Navy's Third Fleet flagship, the battleship *Missouri*, in the middle of Tokyo Bay on September 2, 1945. Here, MacArthur signs off on the official documents after the Japanese government officials in attendance signed the terms of surrender. BELOW: Joyful U.S. Navy officers and men celebrate the news of Japan's official surrender by posing with a copy of the *Stars and Stripes* newspaper that announced that fact to the world.

* On this day the 4th estate went into a frenzy of exultation. Robert Trout on CBS typified the general reaction as he cried out, "The war is over! The war is over! I repeat the war is over! Behind him CBS employees cheered and laughed. We laughed and cheered again. "The Second World War is Over!" Everyone born on or after this date in 1948 are part of the post war generation. JZ

## Suggested Reading

Belote, James H., and William M. Belote, *Corregidor: The Saga of a Fortress.* New York: Harper & Row, 1967.

Brown, David, *Carrier Operations in World War II, Vol. II: The Pacific Navies.* London: Ian Allan, 1974.

Dupuy, R. Ernest, *The Compact History of the United States Army.* New York: Hawthorn Books, 1961.

Fuchida, Mitsuo, and Masatake Okumiya, *Midway, The Battle that Doomed Japan.* New York: Ballantine Books, 1968.

Griffith, Samuel B. II, *The Battle for Guadalcanal.* New York: Ballantine Books, 1963.

Ito, Masanori, with Roger Pineau, *The End of the Imperial Japanese Navy.* New York: W. W. Norton & Company, 1956.

Lockwood, Charles A., and Hans Christian Adamson, *Battle of the Philippine Sea.* Thomas Y. Crowell Company, 1967.

MacArthur, Douglas, *Reminiscences.* New York: McGraw-Hill Book Company, 1964.

Morison, Samuel Eliot, *The Two-Ocean War: A Short History of the United States Navy in the Second World War II.* New York: Little, Brown, 1963.

Potter, E.B., *Nimitz.* Annapolis, Md.: Naval Institute Press, 1976.

Potter, Jonn Deane, *Yamamoto: The Man Who Menaced America.* New York: Viking, 1965.

Smith, S.E., ed., *The United States Marine Corps in World War II.* New York: Ace Books, 1973.

Sunderman, James F., ed., *World War II in the Air: The Pacific.* New York: Franklin Watts, Inc., 1962.

Toland, John, *The Rising Sun.* New York: Random House, 1970.

Wohlstetter, Robert, *Pearl Harbor: Warning and Decision.* Stanford University Press, 1962.

## Selected Military and Ship Museums
(With artifacts on display pertaining to the War in the Pacific)

Aircraft Carrier *Hornet* Museum and Foundation
P.O. Box 460
Alameda, Calif. 94501
Phone: (510) 521-8448
Fax: (510) 521-8327
Website: www.usshornetmuseum.org

Aircraft Carrier *Yorktown*
Patriots Point Naval & Maritime Museum
40 Patriots Point Road
Mount Pleasant, S.C. 29469
Phone: (808) 884-2727
Fax: (808) 881-4232
Website: www.state.sc.us/patpt

Battleship *Alabama*
Battleship Memorial Park
P.O. Box 65
Mobile, Ala. 36601
Phone: (334) 433-2703
Fax: (334) 433-2777
Website: www.mof.mobile.al.us

Battleship *Massachusetts*
Battleship Cove
Fall River, Mass. 02721
Phone: (508) 678-1100 or (800) 533-3194
Fax: (508) 674-5597
Website: battleshipcove.com

Battleship *North Carolina*
P.O. Box 480
Wilmington, N.C. 28402
Phone: (910) 251-5797
Fax: (910) 251-5807
Website: city-info.com/battleship/main.html

*Intrepid* Sea-Air-Space Museum
Pier 86
West 46th Street & 12th Ave
New York, N.Y. 10036
Phone: (212) 245-0072
Fax: (212) 957-3708
Website: www.intrepidmuseum.com

LVT Museum
AAS Bn MCB
Box 555041
Camp Pendleton, Calif. 92055-5041
Phone: (760) 725-2073
Fax: (760) 725-2474

Marine Corps Air-Ground Museum
MCCDC
Quantico, Va. 22134-5001
Phone: (703) 784-2606
Website: www.usmc-history.org/airground

National Museum of Naval Aviation
Building 3465
Pensacola Naval Air Station
Pensacola, Fla. 32508
Phone: (904) 452-3604
Website: www.pcola.com/navy.html

San Diego Aerospace Museum
2001 Pan American Plaza
Balboa Park
San Diego, Calif. 92101
Phone: (619) 234-8291
Fax: (619) 233-4526
Website: aerospacemuseum.org

U.S. Marine Corps Historical Center
Building 58
Washington Naval Yard
901 M Street, S.E.
Washington, D.C. 20374-5060
Phone: (202) 433-0780
Website: www.usmc.mil/
historical.nsf/general+information?openview&count=9999

U.S. Navy Museum
Washington Navy Yard
901 M Street, S.E.
Washington, D.C. 20374-5060
Phone: (202) 433-4882
Fax: (202) 433-8200
Website:www.history.navy.mil/branches/nhcorg8.htm

USS *Lexington* Museum on the Bay
2914 N. Shoreline Blvd.
Corpus Christi, Texas 78402
Phone: (512) 888-4873
Fax: (512) 883-8361
Website: usslexington.com

# Photo Credits

**Courtesy of The Michael Green Collection:** pp. 8, 15, 16–17, 19 top, 19 bottom, 21, 22, 24, 28, 31 top, 32, 36 top, 36 bottom, 37, 38, 42–43, 44, 45 bottom, 46–47, 59, 64, 65, 67 bottom, 71 bottom, 72, 74, 75, 76, 77, 78–79, 83, 85 top, 85 bottom, 86, 87, 88, 89, 94, 95, 99 right, 101, 102, 104–105, 106–107, 108, 109 top, 112, 113 top, 113 bottom, 123 right

**Archive Photos:** pp. 17 right, 29, 31 bottom, 46, 71 top, 115, 121

**FPG International:** pp. 92–93, 96 left, 96–97, 98–99, 100

**Corbis:** pp. 9, 26–27, 35 right, 40, 49, 50, 51, 52 left, 52–53, 54, 60, 61 top, 61 bottom, 67 top, 68, 69, 73, 90, 103, 117 right, 119, 121

**Digital Stock:** pp. 2–3, 4–5, 6–7, 12–13, 18, 24, 39, 54, 55, 56–57, 62–63, 66, 78 left, 80–81, 84, 109 bottom, 110–111, 114, 116–117, 120, 122–123

**National Archives and Records Administration:** pp. 23, 41, 70–71

**San Diego Aerospace Museum:** pp. 33, 45 top, 48, 91

# Illustration Credits

©**Steve Arcella:** pp. 10–11, 14, 30, 34–35, 82;
©**George Bisharat:** pp. 20, 25, 54–55, 58, 118–119

Every effort has been made to ascertain and correctly credit the copyright holders and/or owners for all images appearing in this book. The publisher will correct mistaken credits and include any omitted credits in all future editions.

# Index